King of Scotland James V

Two Ancient Scottish Poems

King of Scotland James V

Two Ancient Scottish Poems

ISBN/EAN: 9783337006884

Printed in Europe, USA, Canada, Australia, Japan

Cover: Foto ©Thomas Meinert / pixelio.de

More available books at **www.hansebooks.com**

TWO

ANCIENT SCOTTISH POEMS;

THE

GABERLUNZIE-MAN,

AND

CHRIST's KIRK ON THE GREEN.

WITH NOTES AND OBSERVATIONS.

BY

JOHN CALLANDER, ESQ. OF CRAIGFORTH.

> By ftrange chanellis, fronteris, and forelandis,
> Uncouth coiftis, and mony vilfum ftrandis,
> Now goith our barge —— G. DOUGLAS.

EDINBURGH:

PRINTED BY J. ROBERTSON.
SOLD BY J. BALFOUR, W. CREECH, AND C. ELLIOT,
EDINBURGH; DUNLOP AND WILSON, GLAS-
GOW; ANGUS AND SON, ABERDEEN;
W. ANDERSON, STIRLING; AND
A. DONALDSON, LONDON.

M,DCC,LXXXII.

TO THE HONOURABLE

SIR DAVID DALRYMPLE, BART.

LORD HAILES,

ONE OF THE SENATORS OF THE COLLEGE

OF JUSTICE.

MY LORD,

IN addresses of this sort, it is almost equally difficult to avoid the servile tone of flattery, as to suppress the honest feelings of the heart, while we speak to those we love and esteem. Happily for me, the public and private character of LORD HAILES will ever secure the author of the following observations from an imputation he disdains, while he gladly embraces the opportunity of presenting this little tract to the person who can best judge, whether an attempt to replace the Etymology of

A   our

our ancient language on a rational and ftable bafis, deferves any attention from the public.

Your Lordfhip has permitted me to look to you, as the patron and guide of my refearches; and it is a poor return to this condefcenfion I now make, in fubfcribing myfelf,

MY LORD,

Your Lordfhip's much obliged,

And moſt faithful humble fervant,

JO. CALLANDER.

CRAIG-FORTH, *April 2.*
1781.

INTRODUCTION.

WE have publiſhed theſe little poems, which tradition aſcribes to James the Fifth of Scotland, with a few notes, as a ſpecimen of the advantages which Etymology may derive from comparing thoſe called *original*, and *ſiſter* languages, and their various dialects. The ſcience of Etymology has, of late years, fallen into diſrepute, rather, I believe, from the ignorance or negligence of ſome of its profeſſed admirers, than becauſe it is of little utility or importance to the Republic of Letters. But many attempts, and ſometimes with ſuccefs, have been made in this kind of inveſtigation. The *Dutch* has been illuſtrated by the *Friſian* and *Teutonic*; the *Engliſh* by the *Anglo-Saxon*; and the *German* has been explained, with much labour and care, by Wachter, and others, from the ancient monuments of the Francs, Goths, and Alamanni. The learned Ihre, Profeſſor at Upſal,

6   INTRODUCTION.

Turks write it *ma*. Gael. *mana*. Gr. μηνη, and Æol. μανα. Dan. *maane*. Alam. *mano*. In the ancient Arabic *manat*. Hebr. *meni*, in Ifa. 66. ii. and the Americans of Virginia fay *manith*, and in the Malabar dialect *mena*, a month. From *man* the Greeks formed μανια, madnefs, fuppofed to be occafioned by the influence of the moon. Hence our *maniac*, a madman; *Menuet*, *minuet*, facred dance, and of very high antiquity, reprefenting the movements of the fun and moon. The primitive *mun*, pronounced *man*, fignifies the *hand* and a *fign*. Hence *mon*, *men*, *man*, are applied to fun and moon, alfo to denote every thing relative to *figns*. Hence Lat. *manus*, and our *month*, &c.

Inftead of carrying on our refearches into the many other collateral meanings of this word, we fhall amufe our readers with another, fhewing that the fame principle of univerfality in language prevails in all.

MALADY.—Hebr. *malul*, evil, chagrin, grief; *moul*, patience. Perf. *mall*, evil. Hebr. *mulidan*, to fuffer. Arab. *mel*, patience. Celt. *mal*, bad, corrupt. Hence Lat. *malum* ; Fr. *mal; malade; maladerie*, an hofpital ; the *malanders*, a difeafe to which horfes are fubject; *malice*, *malignity*.

Lat.

Lat. B. *male-aftrofus, ill-ftarred,* as Shakefpeare has it, Othello, Act V.

Had the laborious Johnfon been better acquainted with the Oriental tongues, or had he even underftood the firft rudiments of the Northern languages from which the Englifh and Scots derive their origin, his bulky volumes had not prefented to us the melancholy truth, That unwearied induftry, devoid of fettled principles, avails only to add one error to another.

Junius, Skinner, and Lye, though far fuperior to Mr Johnfon in their knowledge of the origin of our language, yet, in tracing its foundation, feldom go farther back than the Celtic, and Ulphila's Gothic verfion of part of the New Teftament. Nay, the elegant and learned Ihre tells us plainly, that it is unjuft to demand any thing further. But ftill the queftion recurs to an inquifitive reader, Whence were thefe Celtic and Gothic terms formed? Every fmatterer in Etymology knows that the Greek and Latin are modern tongues, when compared to the Oriental and Celtic dialects; and the blundering attempts of Euftathius, the author of the Etymologicon Magnum, Varro, and Feftus, prove, beyond a doubt, that thefe writers were equally ignorant of the true meaning of their

mother

mother tongues, and of the originals from whence they were derived. Misled by those blind guides, we find Vossius and Skinner very gravely asserting, that *Venus* is formed *a veniendo*, quia omnibus venit ; *vulgus*, a volvendo ; *malus*, from the Greek μελας, black, and μαλακος ; *manus* from *munus* ; and *mons*, a mountain, *a movendo*, quia minimè movetur ; *mare*, quod amarum sit ; *muscle* of the body, from *mus* ; and *musquet*, from the Greek μοσχος, a calf.

It were easy to swell this catalogue, which any of our readers may augment at their pleasure from *every* page of *every* Lexicographer, ancient and modern.

Of all the Nothern dialects none has been more neglected than the Scotch, though it transmits to us many works of genius both in poetry and prose ; and also some glossaries, which are not unuseful in pointing out the affinity of the ancient Scotch with its kindred dialects. Of these, the largest is that annexed to Bishop Douglas's version of the Æneid. But it wants many words which actually exist in that translation, and a great many more are so distorted by false derivations, that they only serve to multiply our doubts.

Our language, as it is at present spoken by the common people in the Lowlands, and as it

appears

appears in the writings prior to the seventeenth century, furnishes a great many observations, highly deserving the attention of those who wish to be acquainted with the Scandinavian dialects in general, or the terms used by our ancestors in their jurisprudence and poetry, in particular. Many of those serve materially to illustrate the genius, the manners, and customs of our forefathers. In Scotland, the Old Saxon dialect, which came over with *Octa* and *Nebrissa*, the founders of the Northumbrian kingdom, has maintained its ground much longer than in England, and in much greater purity. This must be owing to the later cultivation of this part of the island, and its less frequent communication with strangers. In South Britain, the numerous swarms of Normans and French, who followed William, and the Plantagenets, soon made their language that of the bar, and of the court. At the same time, the long wars with France, and the extensive possessions of the English on that part of the continent, entirely changed not only the orthography, but also the pronunciation of the original Saxon; nor do we hesitate to say, what we shall soon endeavour to prove, that we, in Scotland, have preserved the original tongue, while it has been mangled, and almost defaced, by our southern neighbours.

It is an undoubted fact, that the original language of this whole Ifland was the Celtic, now fplit into the feveral dialects of the *Gaelic, Welch*, and *Armoric*. In the prefent Scotch, we fee indeed a few traces of this ancient tongue, which the inhabitants left behind them, when they fled for refuge to the mountains of Scotland and Wales; but thefe are very eafily diftinguifhed from the now prevailing language of the country. In like manner we difcover to this day, in the German, many marks of the fame original, which were infufed into it by the neighbouring Belgæ and Gauls, the pofterity of the ancient Celts, by whom this Ifland was originally peopled. *Sufmilch* has proved this from the likenefs of many German and Armoric words. Many more examples might be adduced from the Gaelic, in which the radical word is often preferved, though loft in all the dialects of the German language. Of this number is the word *fchleufe*, the root of which is only to be found in the Welch *Llaw*, the arm, or the hand. From this word was formed *Llawes*, which has been adopted into all the German dialects, in the fame manner as *manica* from *manus*, or the Irifh word *braccaile*, a bracelet, from *brac*, the arm, and *caile*, an ornament or covering. The word *treten*, has alfo greatly

puzzled

INTRODUCTION.

puzzled the German etymologists, though it seems naturally derived from the Irish *troed*, the foot, whence also comes our word *tread*.

The intimate connection of the Scots with the Teutonic, German, Islandic, and other northern dialects, appears, first, from the similarity of found, and enunciation. This is principally to be remarked in the found of the vowels, which retain the same uniform tones in the broad Scotch, that they do in the languages above mentioned : whereas the singular caprice of the English pronunciation has varied and confounded them beyond the comprehension of rule. The German guttural pronunciation of *ch*, *g*, *gh*, is quite natural to a Scotchman, who forms the words *eight*, *light*, *fight*, *bought*, &c. exactly as his northern neighbours, and as the Germans do. How much the English have deviated from this, we may see from the few following examples.

German.	Scots.	English.
Beide,	Baith,	Both.
Eide,	Aith,	Oath.
Kiste,	Kist,	Chest.
Meiste,	Maist,	Most.
Brennen,	Bren,	Burn.
Gehe,	Gae,	Go, &c.

INTRODUCTION.

We have to obferve, in the fecond place, that our language contains many words which were never admitted into the Englifh dialect. Thefe, a few excepted, which are derived from the Gaelic, are either pure German, or Scandinavian. We have annexed a few examples from our Scoto-Gothic gloffary as a fpecimen.

Scots.		German, &c.
Blate,	Bel.	Blode.
Dech,		Deeg.
Barm, yeft,	B.	Barm.
Kail,	G.	Kohl.
Coft,		Koeft.
Bikker,	G.	Becher.
Sicker,		Sicher.
Kemp,		Kampfen.
Haus,	G.	Hals.
Mutch,	G.	Mutz.
Skaith,	G.	Schade.
Slough, fkin,	B.	Slu.
Spill,	B.	Spillen.
Red, advife,	G.	Rathen.
Lift, fky,	G.	Luft.
Tig, touch gently,	B.	Ticken.
Forloffen,	G.	Weglaufen.
Bruick,	G.	Brauchan.
Reek,		Rauch.
Bouk,	G.	Baugh, the belly.
Fie, cattle,	G.	Vieh.
Kummer,	G.	Kummer, forrow.
Krummy, crooked,	G.	Krumm.

Fremd,

INTRODUCTION. 13

Scots.	German, &c.	
Fremd,	G.	Fremd, ſtrange.
Low, flame,	G.	Lohe, flame.
Leglen,	G.	Leghel, a milking-pail.
Win,	G.	Wohnen, to dwell.
Yammer,	G.	Jammern, to complain.
Keek,	B.	Kieken.
Girn,	Iſl.	Girnd, deſire, anger.
Muil,	Iſl.	Molld, pulvis.
Egg,	Iſl.	Egg, acies.
Awn,	Goth.	Aigan, to poſſeſs—*Aigin*, my own.
Elden,	Iſl.	Eldur, fire.
Etter and ettercap,	Iſl.	Eitur, poiſon, venom.
Dill,	Iſl.	Dil, to conceal.
Ern,	Iſl.	Ernur, large hawk.

Theſe may ſuffice, though it were eaſy to add more examples.

The uſe of inveſtigating our Scottiſh dialect, will alſo appear from its retaining many radical words, which are either totally loſt in its ſiſter languages, or which are no longer enounced in the primitive ſounds. In this number is *gear*, or *gier*, which ſignifies dreſs, furniture, wealth. This word, like the Greek αιγις, denoting originally *a goat-ſkin*, afterwards *a ſhield*, and laſtly the *ſacred ſhield* of Minerva, has greatly enlarged its primitive ſignification. From the original meaning of the Iſlandic *gera*, a ſheep-ſkin, this word came to ſignify covering, dreſs, ornament, goods,

goods, riches; cattle being all thefe to the moſt ancient nations. Now this word is uſed by our writers, in all theſe acceptations; and, though no longer found in the German, yet it is the fruitful mother of many ancient and modern words in that language. From it are evidently derived *hauſegeraeth*, the Saxon *gerada*, and the Swediſh *gerad* and *gerd*, tribute paid both in goods and money; the etymon of which neither Spegel nor Ihre underſtood:--- (Vide Ihre, Lex. in *gerd*, *utgerd*). The word *graith*, in our language ſignifying utenſils and furniture of all kinds, is from the ſame origin; as alſo the German *gier*, a miſer; *gieren*, to deſire anxiouſly; *geirig*, covetous; *gern*, willing-ly, whence our *yearn*, with many others of the ſame family, the ſignification being changed from the *object* itſelf to the *deſire* of poſſeſſing it, and afterwards enlarged to expreſs any *deſire* in general, in the ſame manner as in Engliſh the word *liquoriſh*, from *liquor*, in its primary ſenſe firſt denoted the deſire of *drinking*, and after-wards any *luſtful deſire*. Our word *gar*, make, prepare, is another word not found at preſent in the German language, in its original meaning. But from it come the words *gar*, ready; *garven*, to prepare and curry leather; with a great many more in the old and pure German dialect; and

in

in the Alammanic *garuuin, garuuen,* whence *garue,* ready, prepared; the Iflandic *giorwer,* ready made; and in the ancient Runic Infcriptions, *gjarva, kiarva,* whence our *carve,* to cut up, *i. e.* prepare meat for eating. The Welfh fay *kervio,* and the Gaels *corrbham.* Cafaubon and Stephanus were certainly driven to the laft extremity, while they bring in this word from the Greek εγκυρα, or κυρα, a picture. But with thefe writers, the moft extravagant conjectures often fupply the want of folid principles.

To mention only one inftance more; our word *grean,* the muzzle or upper-lip of cattle, is the only root from whence the German *grynen,* to laugh, can be derived, the etymology of which has given rife to a variety of conjectures. Our *girn,* and the Englifh *grin,* are from the fame root.

Thefe few remarks may fuffice to fhew the great ufefulnefs and importance of inveftigating the terms and phrafes of our ancient language, fince thefe not only tend to elucidate the ancient manners and cuftoms of our remote anceftors, but alfo throw much light on its fifter-dialects of the North; by which we mean all thofe fpoken from the heads of the Rhine, and of the Danube, to the fartheft extremities of Scandinavia and Iceland.

It

It is high time that something of this kind were attempted to be done, before the present Engliſh, which has now for many years been the written language of this country, ſhall baniſh our Scottiſh tongue entirely out of the world.

We cannot conclude theſe curſory remarks without congratulating our readers on the eſtabliſhment of a Society, which promiſes to revive a taſte for the ſtudy of national antiquity. The worthy nobleman to whoſe truly patriotic ſpirit it owes its inſtitution, and the gentlemen aſſociated for ſo laudable a purpoſe, it is hoped, will look with indulgence on this poor attempt to ſecond their endeavours, in reſtoring and explaining the ancient language of Scotland.

THE
GABERLUNZIE-MAN.

I.

THE pauky auld Carle came o'er the lee,
Wi' mony gude eens and days to mee,
Saying,

Gaberlunzie] This word is compounded of *Gaber, Gabber*, a Wallet or Bag, and *Lunzie*, loin, *i. e.* the man who carries the wallet on his back, an itinerant mechanic, or tinker, who carries in his bag the implements of his trade, and strolls about the country mending pots and kettles. In such disguises as this James V. (as is said) used to go about the country, and to mingle, unknown, with the meanest of his subjects. These frolicksome excursions often gave birth to little amorous adventures, which our witty Monarch made the subjects of his song, as he was second to none of his age in the sciences of poetry and music.

The root of the word *gab* is the Celt. *cab*, signifying to contain. Hence Scot. *gab*, the mouth, which contains our food; English *gobbet*, a morsel; the French *gober*, to swallow, and *gosier*, the throat. The large barks on Loch-Lomond for carrying wood, are called *gaberts*. From *gab*, and *gab*, come Englifh *gabble*; and *gabbing* is ufed by Douglas for idle talking, Prologue to I. Æn. p. 6. v. 43. Rud. Edit.—and laft line of leaf 3. Lond. Edit. 4to, 1553.

" Quhilk is nae gabbing fouthly, nor no lye."

In the fame fenfe, Ifl. *gabb*; Ludibrium, *gabba*, to deride; A. Sax. *gabban*, and many more words of the fame import, *gaggle*, *gaffer*, and Old Fr. *gaber*, *gabbaffer*, to mock; *gabatine*, mockery; Iflandic *gamman*, drollery; Gal. *geubbeth*, falfehood; and *gaw*, *caw*, *gab*, cheating; Old Fr. *ganelon*, a traitor. We have collected thefe words from various languages, as they not only explain the primitive idea of the word *gaber*, which none of our Etymologifts have done, but prove what we fhall every moment have occafion to fhew, that the radical term once afcertained, throws light on all its derivatives, which are eafily reducible to it, though fcattered far diftant from each other, among the various dialects ufed by different nations. To this family belongs Lat. *capio*, whence our *capacity*, *capture*; the Scots *cap*, a drinking veffel; *cab*, a meafure, mentioned in the Verfion of the Old Teftament; and many more, all including the idea of *capacity*, or *content*; as *cabin*, Belg. *kaban*; Welfh, *cab*, *caban*, all fignifying the fame thing; Gr. καπανη; Lat. *cabana*, *cabbage*, from the form of its top, refembling a bafon or large cup, which has much puzzled Junius; Lat. *cavus*, our *cave*, and the Fr. and Engl. *cabinet*.

Lunzie] We have elfewhere obferved, with Mr Ruddiman, that the Z, by the old Scots writers, is always ufed in the beginning of the fyllable for the Englifh Y. The reafon is, that the figure Z much refembles the Saxon G, which the Englifh often change into Y, as *yard* from *geard*; *yea* from *gea*;

year

year from *gear*, &c. Thus *Yetland* is by us written *Zetland*, and *ye, year, young* ; *ze, zere, zyng ; ranzies, fenzies*, for *reins, feigns*, and the like. This we remark once for all. In other fifter dialects Z has the force of S. Thus Bel. *zour*, four ; *zuid*, fouth ; *zon*, fun ; Slav. *zakar*, fugar ; Ital. *zanni*, Gr. ϛα:νοι, and in the Bar. Gr. *7ϛανοι*, buffoons, whence our *zany*.

Lunzie] Lung, loin, lunzie ; *bene*, the thigh bone. In Swed. *lend, land*, the loin. In the Laws of Gothland, cap. 23. 4. *Synes lend oc lyndtr* ; fi appareant lumbi et pudenda. They alfo write it *Ljumske*; Ihre, in voce. Ifl. *lend, boh, ledwi*. Ger. *lenden* and *lanken*, and hence our *flank*. Welfh, *Llwyn*; and in Finland, *landet*, the loin. Ital. *longia*; Fr. *longe*; Scot. *lend*. Vide Not. S. Kirk. St. From the ancient Goth. *Ljumske* ; the Lat. *lumbus* ; Dan. *ljuske* ; whence our *lisk*. The primitive is *Lat, Let*, broad, extended; whence the Gr. πλατυς, and the Latin *latus*.

Thus the *Gaberlunzie-man* literally fignifies the man who bears a bag, or wallet, on his back or loins ; a pedlar ; Scot. a *pack-man*.

STANZA I.

VER. 1. *Pauky*] Sly, cunning, Bel. *Paiken*, to coax or wheedle. Douglas, p. 238, v. 37.
Prattis are repute policie, and perrellus *paukis*.

Auld] Old Ger. *alt*, as *eald*. Ifl. *aldradur*. Dan. *Eeld*. Scot. *eild*. Cafaubon brings this from εωλος, vetus, and Lye from αλδεω, augeo ; as if our anceftors had no word to exprefs old age, till they got it from the Greeks. But this is indeed an old wife's tale. The primitive *E* denotes exiftence; every thing that lives. Hence *Eve* is called emphatically, the mother of all living. Lat. *eft*. Fr. *etre*, being, *effentia*, whence our *effence*, what conftitutes the *being* of that thing. Hence Hebrew

20   THE GABERLUNZIE-MAN.

Hebrew *hei*, life, and *God* emphatically; i. e. *He who lives.* *heie*, to live, life itſelf. Arab. *hei—hi*, to live, to be glad. In Zend, *gueie*, ſoul, life. This word furniſhes a remarkable example of the truth of our general principle, explained in the preface, and therefore we hope the reader will allow us to trace it a little further. The aſpirate H, in the northern dialects, is changed into W, and Qu, and hence Swed. *weet*, *wight*, living animal; Engl. and Scot. *wight*; Goth, *qwick*, lively; *ewicka*, quicken, quick-ſilver, from its lively motion. In Sued. *qwick-ſilſwer*. The Latins uſed the V, and ſo formed *vita, vivere, vivax, victus, victo, vis, vigor, vigeo*, and a thouſand more; as alſo the derivatives we have adopted from that language, *vivacity, violent, vivid*, &c. Voſſius, able to get no further than the Greek, deduces *vita* from Βιοτη: but Βιος, life; Βια, violence, Βιακοπαι, Βιοω, all come from one primitive, as alſo Gr. ις, the *vis* of the Latins, ισχυς, ισχυα, ισχυρος, only by ſuppreſſing the aſpirate. In the more ancient dialects of Scandinavia, we find the ſame word denoting the ſame objects; Teuton. *vuith*. Iſl. *vætir*. a Sax. *vught, vight*, all ſign. animals, living creatures; and the Alam. *quick, quickr*. Old German *queck*. Dan. *queg*, living, animal, every thing alive. Suab. *vich, viech*, animal. From the ſame ſource we formed *wife*. Bel. *wyf*. Swed. *wif*. Suab. *wib*, all ſignifying *woman*, mother of a family.

Thus we have followed this word from the remoteſt Eaſt, to the fartheſt extremities of the Weſt and North. Such coincidences of ſound and meaning, demonſtrate that language is no arbitrary thing, nor etymology that fallacious ſcience it has been called, by thoſe who find it more eaſy to decide in haſte, than to examine at leiſure.

Carle] The true ſpelling is *karl* in all the Scythian dialects, in which it denotes a *man*, or *warrior*. The primitive is *car—kar*, ſtrong. This root we have preſerved in the Armenian,

THE GABERLUNZIE-MAN.

menian, in which *car*, *poffe*, *valere*, et *carol*, *potens*. Not attending to the univerfality of language, the learned Ihre did not fee the juftnefs of this Etymology. From *kair*, *kar*, the Mefogothic, *vair*, a man; whence the Lat. *vir*, *vira*, a woman, as from the Gothic *kas*, they formed *vas*, which Voffius could make nothing of, though he has flung together every paffage almoft, where this word occurs. From *karl* are formed the Alamm. *karl*; Ger. *kerl*; A. S. *ceorl*; Ifl. *karl*; L. B. *Carolus*, *karlus*. Vid. Cange Glofs. in V. From *kerl*, Sued. *karlklader*, men's clothes; *karlſmather*, and *karlſwag*, the highway; and in the old Gothic laws *karlſbo*, man's habitation. The word *karl* is oppofed to *gaffe*, a youth; the former denoting a man of ripe age. We find that of old, in the Gothic, as now with us, *karl*, and *carl*, were ufed to fignify people of a low rank, fuch as farmers, mechanics, &c. In the old laws, (ap. Ihre glofs. Vol. I. P. 1033,) *karl oc konung*, plebs et princeps; and in Gothr. Saga, cap. 86, *opter that I karls hufi er ej er in congs ranni*, oft do we meet in a cottage, what we feek in vain in the palaces of kings. In general, *karl* is ufed to fignify a *husband*; and in Sweden the country-women call their hufbands *min-karl*. In the Swedifh tongue the gander is called *gas-karl*. So in Engl. a *carle-cat*, is the male of that fpecies. The Anglo-Saxons fay *ceorl*, for a hufband, and *ceorlian*, to marry.

As this word was commonly ufed to fignify *ruſtics*, the Enlifh from it formed *churl*, *churlifh*. In the A. S. *ceorlborin* is a man meanly born; *ceorlife*, a ruftic; *ceorlife hlaf*, loaf made of the fecond flour. In Dutch, *kaerle* a ruftic; whence the Italian phrafe, *a la carlona*, like a ruftic, ill-bred. The Welch *carl* has the fame meaning. As *karl*, all over the north, denotes an *elderly man*, from it we have formed *carling*, an old woman of the loweft caft, a word which occurs in all our poets.

The

Saying, Gudewife, for zour courtefie,
Will zee ludge a filly poor man.

The

The Bar. Lat. *Carolus*, and our *Charles*, come from the fame origin, a name of high antiquity among the Germans, from whom we borrowed the name of the conftellation *Charles's wain*, in Gothic *Karlwagn*, and in Sax. *Carleas wagn*; Dan. *Karlvogn*. This proves the ignorance of thofe who will have this name given to thefe ftars in honour of Charles the Great, which was in general ufe many ages before Charlemain was born. The Welch alfo call this conftellation *Cart Wyn*.

VER. I. *Lee*, or *lea*] An unplowed field, or a field formerly under corn, and afterwards laid down in grafs. Primitive *la*, and *le*, fignify broad, extended. A. S. *lea, leag, leah*. Old Ger. *la, lo, lohe*. Goth. *lee*, which Ihre explains, *locus tempeftatibus fubductus*; whence our *lown*, calm. In the northern parts of Germany, we have it in many names of places, as *Oldefloh, Kartla, Lohagen*, &c. vide Grupen Antiq. Van Den Bonnen. P. 556. Ifl. *logn*, and Goth. *lugn*, fign. *calm*. The Hebr. *lech*, denotes a meadow, green, verdure; and the Polifh *leka* is the fame, for all thefe are derived from the fame root, *la*. The Celtic and Gallic *las*, fign. grafs. Welch *Llys*; *bas*, Brett. *luzavan*. Hence *Lucern*, a fpecies of grafs growing abundantly in Switzerland. The Canton of *Lucern* has its name from this plant, not the plant from it, as the high antiquity of the word proves.

VER. 3. *Gudewife*] Properly the mother of a family; Goth. *wif*, a woman, a married woman. A. S. id. Ger. *weif*. This by fome has been derived from *wifwa*, to weave; by others from *wif*, or *hwif*, a woman's head-drefs,

in

THE GABERLUNZIE-MAN. 23

in the fame way as the Swedes fay *gyrdel* and *linda*, the belt, and girdle for the *man* and the *woman*. They alfo ufe *hatt* and *hætta*, the hat and cap, in the fame fenfe. But the true primitive of this word is E, life, exiftence; whence *Eve*, the general mother of mankind; Arab. *heih*, the female fex, alfo modefty. This word *heih*, pronounced *hai*, gave birth to the ancient formulary of marriage among the Romans, *Ubi tu eras Caius* (fays the woman) *ego ero Caia*. None of their writers tell us any thing of the origin of thefe *verba concepta*. *Caia* was in reality a title of honour given to the Roman matrons, anfwering to that of *Thane*, ufed by the Etrufcans; whence, it would feem, the Italian *Donna* came. So Pliny, l. 8. cap. 48. tells us that *Caia Kaikilia*, wife to the elder Tarquin, was called in the Hetrufcan, *Thana Quilis*. He and *hei*, the primitive, with the change of the H into G, the eafieft of all tranfpofitions, formed in Greek γαω, whence γεγαω, to generate, γενεσις, γενος, race, family; γονευς, parent; γυνν, a wife; Lat. *genus, gigno, gens*; Chin. *gin*; Celt. *gen*, a man; Greenl. *kora*; Ifl. Teut. Dan. *kona;* Cuen. *quin*, woman; and our *quean* and *queen;* Gaelic, *quenaft*, to marry; Slav. *fyena*, a woman; and Fr. *guenon*, the female monkey.

From the fame root the *Earth*, the *nourifher* of men and animals, is, in every language, called by the fame appellation. Chinefe *chi*; Gael. *gwe*; Zend *gweth, enanm;* Pehlvi *gue, ha*, the world; Gael. *gwaed*, riches, goods produced by the Earth; Celtic, *gueth*, a poor man, one deftitute of thefe goods, compofed of *gue*, the Earth, and the negative termination *th;* Ancient Gr. Αια, γαια, γεα, and γη, the Earth. Hence we can eafily trace the origin of the Latin *egeo* and *egenus*, which literally fignifies *to be without ground*, to be deftitute of the fruits of the Earth. *Inops*, from the negative

in

in and *ops,* the ancient appellative of our common mother, as in that verse of the old poet Accius, Ap. Prisc. Lib. 7.

" Quorum genitor fertur esse *ops* gentibus."

Plautus Cistellar:

" Itaque me ops opulenta illius avia, imo mater quidem."

How little Vossius and Isidorus knew the real origin of the Latin words, may be seen, apud Voss. Etym. in *Egens*. Nor has Festus succeeded a whit better, when he says, *Egens, velut exgens,* cui ne gens quidem sit reliqua ; and yet these writers are called *Etymologists*. We leave them amidst these futile derivations, and proceed to observe, that from this primitive *he,* life, nourishment, are derived a number of Celtic words, all of the same import ; as *hei,* our *hay,* food of animals produced by the Earth; *heize,* barley; *hai,* trees, a forest ; *hei, wei,* pasturage, hunting ; *he* and *kai,* habitation, literally the place *where we live.* And as those who abound in goods are, or should be *cheerful,* hence Gr. γαω, rejoice ; Chinese, *gao,* to laugh or be glad; Celt. *gae,* id. Latin, *gavisus, gaudere ;* the French and our *gay,* and Scot. *gauf*.

We have extended our remarks on this word, as it strongly confirms our hypothesis relating to the universality of the primitive language, and the existence of its elementary parts, in every dialect spoken by men, even at this day, from the remotest parts of the East, to the farthest limits of the North and West. In all these languages, we have seen that this root, exceedingly simple in itself, has proved the fruitful mother of many families in every quarter of the globe. These may shew, that the primæval language was not *eradicated* at Babel, but only *split* into a great variety of dialects, as the sacred Historian informs us; and that the several languages now in use, are so far from being formed by the tribes who

speak

The night was cauld, the carle was wat,
And down azont the ingle he fat ;

My

ſpeak them, that they are only branches of that primæval tree, which flouriſhed long before the deluge.

We might eaſily accumulate more proofs of the truth of our leading principle, were we to add the Hebr. *eia*, being ; Indian *he ;* Perſ. *aiſt ;* Gr. ις; Lat. *eſt ;* Baſq. *iſan ;* Celt. *es ;* Teuton. *iſh, ys ;* Ital. *e ;* and Engliſh *is :* But theſe we ſhall reſerve for our Gloſſary, in compiling of which we have already made ſome progreſs.

VER. 4. *Silly.*—Simple, without guile. In old Engliſh *ſely, ſelie.* So Chaucer, Miller's Tale, and Reve's Tale, v. 992. The *Sely Carpenter,* and elſewhere *ſelie-man.* This is quite different from *Sely,* ſign. *holy,* from Goth. *ſalig,* A. S. *ſæl.*

VER. 5. *Cauld.*—In this word we have an inſtance of our following the original orthography. Ulphila writes *calds ;* A. S. *ceald ;* Iſl. *caldur* and *kulde ;* Alam. *kalt ;* Dan. *kuld ;* all ſignifying *cold.*

Wat.—Engl. *wet ;* Prim. *u, au,* water ; Ulph. *wato ;* Goth. *watn ;* Pol. *wat,* humid; A. S. *water;* Alam. *wuaſzar ;* Ger. *waſſer ;* Pol. *wæda ;* Gr. ὕδωρ, which Plato (in Cratylo) allows to be a barbarous word ; and he is in the right, for the Greeks had it from the Celtic. Iſland. *udr* is *water.* Hence Goth. *wattu-ſiktig,* the dropſy, literally the *water-ſickneſs.* From the Iſl. *watſka,* the Engliſh *waſh.* From the ſame origin comes the Swediſh *O,* an Iſland, becauſe ſurrounded with water ; *Aland, Æland,* an Iſland in the Baltic ; *Ho-lland,* literally *a land of waters.* There is a diſtrict in Normandy called *Auge,* for the ſame reaſon. *Eau* has the ſame origin.

D . We

We shall add some other coincidences of language here, in support of our general principle, that the radical words of the first tongue are to be found in dialects spoken by nations, who never had any connection with each other since the dispersion at Babel. These are so numerous, and deviate so little both from the original sound and sense, that it can never be supposed, without the grossest absurdity, to be the effect of chance. Thus the Chinese *ko—hu*, signifies *water* in general, a lake, and *hai*, the sea. The Tartar *Icho*, a river in Siberia; and in the same language, *O-mo*, a lake, literally a *great water*, for *mo* is great. Greek ὕς, water; whence ὕω, to rain, ὕδωρ, ὕδρος, ὕδρια; yet Stephanus and Scapula tell us, that ὕδωρ and ὕω are radical words, not knowing that no radical word ever consisted of two syllables. Indeed, we may venture to assert, that no example can be produced of a true radical word having more than one. The public has lately been told, in very pompous terms, that the Greek language is the work of philosophers, complete and perfect in itself. We can most easily shew, that this wild assertion is so far from being true, that no person, but one utterly devoid of all skill in Etymology and the analogy of language, could have hazarded an hypothesis so replete with absurdity. So far is the Greek tongue from being the work of philosophers, that one of their best philosophers, in one of his (best) dialogues, ingenuously confesses, that he is quite ignorant of the origin of many of the most common words in the language. Such is the word ὕδωρ mentioned above, and a vast number of others, which he, with a true Attic supercilious air, allows to have been borrowed from the Barbarians. True it is, these terms do derive their origin from the Scythians, Thracians, Phrygians, and Celts, whose language existed many ages before Athens was even a poor village. The very meanest of these people, whom he stigmatises with the name of Barbarians, could have informed him of the origin of

ὕδωρ,

ὕδωρ, as well as of many others of which he owns himself equally ignorant. After Plato, it is almost needless to observe, that those who were far inferior to this Athenian in the knowledge of language, were still more unfortunate in their explications. Let every page of Hesychius, Eustathius, Suidas, the Etymologicon Magnum, Tzetzes, Harpocation, and the whole herd of their commentators and lexicographers, bear witness to their ignorance, and account for the disgrace into which the useful study of Etymology has, by their means, fallen among those who have rashly concluded, that because nothing good was done by these Scioli in the profession, therefore nothing better could be done. Let us leave this language of yesterday, said to be formed by philosophers, to the admiration of those profound philosophers, who have told us, that, in certain Islands in the Eastern Ocean, the human race have tails, and whose credulity can digest the account the natives of Attica gave of themselves, pretending that they sprung, like mushrooms, from the very soil on which they dwelt. All these pretenders to the highest antiquity, were outdone in Grecian rhodomontade by the Arcadians, who asserted, that they inhabited their mountainous district long before the moon appeared in the heavens.

We haften to return from a digression, which, we are afraid, many of our learned readers will deem unnecessary; though perhaps others may think, that the hints here thrown out, concerning the Greek tongue, may help to loosen the college-fetters of those, who, from their early youth, have been accustomed to look upon nothing as genuine and valuable, unless found in some of the writers of classic authority; nor any thing expressed with elegance and propriety, unless written in Greek. The chronological blunders of those, who are perpetually deriving Scythian, Tartar, and Celtic words, from a language which did not receive its prefent form, till many centuries after the others were fpoken and cultivated, deferve nothing but contempt.

We have faid that ὕδωρ comes from the primitive Celtic *A—U*, water, liquid. From the fame origin the Latins formed *udus, humidus, humeo, humor, hyems*, literally *the feafon of rains*, concerning which, fee the nothings of Voffius, in *Humor* and *Hyems*. From the fame caufe the 'Υάδες, *Hyades*, derived their name. The primitive *au* was fometimes pronounced *oua* ; whence Fr. *eau*, the Lat. *aqua*, and, with the termination *ter, ouater*, water.

VER. 6. *Azont.*—Beyond. A. S. *begeond, begeondan*. The primitive is *ga—ge*, to *go*, and *on*, forward, or beyond the place one ftood in. Ulphila, *ganga*, to go or walk ; whence our *gang, gae*, and *gete*, way, as in S. G. it is written *ga*. From *ga*, written *ba*, the Greeks formed βαω, βαινω, and all their derivatives. The Englifh *gad-about* is from the fame origin ; and Ihre explains the S. G. *gadda*, capita conferre, ut folent novas res molientes. The fame idea is found in the A. S. *gaderian, gadran* ; Bel. *gaderin* ; whence Engl. *gather;* the Ger. *gatten* and *ehegatten*, married pair. Ulphila, Mark 3. V. *Ja fah gaiddja fitt mangeei*, the people were gathered together. Wherever in the Mæfo Gothic we find the prefix *ga*, it always denotes a *gathering*, or going together. So *gafinthja*, comitatur ; *garanznans*, vicini, from *razn*, a houfe ; *gadailans*, partaker, from *dail*, a part; *galhaiba*, contubernales, from *illaibs*, bread ; Alamm. *caleibo*, literally Eaters of the fame bread, whence Ihre deduces Fr. *compagnon*, companion. The Ifl. *kuon gaudur*, married, is from the fame origin, as Wachter rightly obferves, though Ihre does not approve of this derivation.

VER. 6. *Ingle.*—This word is commonly derived from *ignis*. In our language it denotes a fire on the hearth, or in kilns

THE GABERLUNZIE-MAN.

My dochter's fhouthers he 'gan to clap,
And cadgily ranted and fang.

O kilns and ovens, and is ufed by Douglas in many places. It is likewife preferved in Cumberland, as Ray informs us.

VER. 7. *Clap.*—From the Ifl. and Goth. *klappa*, to clap the hands. Dan. *klappe.* Belg. *klappen, cloppen.* This word is plainly an *onomatapœa*, formed from the found made by clapping the hands. Hence too was formed the Greek κολαπτω, *tundere.* Whence Junius idly derives our word *clap.* The fpeaking by the fingers was an art well known to the ancient Iflanders, who called it *clapruner*, or letters formed by the motion of the hands, vide Worm. Litt. Run. p. 41. The watchmen in Holland carry a wooden inftrument with two leaves, which, by clapping together, produce a great noife; whence thefe night-guardians are called *klappermen.* In the ancient Alammanick, the tongue of a bell is called *clepel;* whence our Scots word to *clep*, or talk idly, repeating the fame thing over and over. The Dutch ufe the verb *klappen*, in the fame fenfe. Goth. *klæk*, infamy, difhonour ; *klæknamn, klækord*, opprobrious language, nicknames. The ingenious and learned profeffor Ihre takes *klæpa*, with great probability, from the primitive *laf*, the hand ; Suiogoth. *lofa, lofwa ;* Welch *llaw ;* whence Scot. *lufe*, the palm of the hand ; and the Latin *vola ;* Welch *lloffi, dyloffi,* to ftroke with the hand. Hefych.

To ftricke, from the fame origin, as alfo *colaphus*, and *alapa*, Bar. Lat. *eclaffa.* In a charter of the year 1285, " Si mulier det ei unum *eclaffa*, non debet bannum." *Cange in voce.*

VER. 8. *Cadgily.*—After the manner of the *cadgers*, or thofe who carry about goods for fale in *cages*, by us called

creels,

II.

O Wow! quo' he, war I as free,
As firſt whan I faw this country,
How blythe and mirry wad I be!
And I wad never think lang.

He

creels, on horſes backs, who uſe to ſing, in order to beguile the tedioufneſs of the way. Prim. *ca, cad, cap*, any thing made for *containing*, as we have already obſerved. Some think it comes from the Gael, *cadhla* I.

VER. 8. *Ranted.*—Made a noiſe. Prim. Hebr. *ran*, to cry. Hence the Latin *rana*, a frog, and French *grenouille*, its diminutive. From hence Gr. γερανος, which Stephanus in Biſuvια explains πικρος ϐατραχος; alſo written γυρινος, γερινος, as Euſtathius obſerves.

STANZA II.

VER. 1. *Wow.*—Interjection, from Ger. *weh*, alas; Iſl. *warla*, with difficulty; Snorro, Tom. 2. P. 102. *Swa warla feck. Brætit* ut ægre dirui poſſit; written alſo *valla, verkunna*, to have pity; and S. G. *warkunna*, id. Douglas p. 158. 27.

" Ut on the wandrand ſpreits *wow* thou cryis."

VER. 3. *Blyth.*—Glad. A. S. *blythe;* Belg. *bly*, id. Ulphila *bleiths*, pitiful. Lucke 6. 36. *Jah Atta iſwara bleiths iſt*, as your father is merciful. In the A. S. it denotes *meek, placid, ſimple*; Iſl. *bluther, bludur*, bland, affable. Hence the A. S. *blithſan, bletſan*, rejoice; whence our *bleſs*. In Douglas it is written *blyith*.

VER. 5.

He grew canty, and fcho grew fain;
But little did her auld minny ken
 What

VER. 5. *Canty.*—Cheerful. Belg. *hantig,* merry. *Een cantiger karl,* a gamefome fellow; and, as cheerfulnefs attends good health, the Chefhire-man fays, *very cant, God yield you,* i. e. very ftrong and lufty. To *cant* too, is ufed for recovering or growing better; Yorkfhire, A health to the goodwife *canting,* recovery after child-bearing. Douglas, *cant,* merry, cheerful; *cant,* the language of gypfies, vid. Spelm. in Egyptiani. Gaelic, *caint,* difcourfe; *canteach,* full of talk. From this Celtic origin comes Lat. *cano,* to fing; Fr. *chanfon, chanter,* &c. Lat. *occento,* de qua voce vide Feft. It would have faved Voffius much labour, had he known the true Etymon.

VER. 5. *Fain.*—Full of wifhes. Douglas writes it *fane,* glad; Ulphila *faginon,* id. Ifl. *feigin;* A. S. *wægn, fægn.* Ulphila thus tranflates the Angel's falutation of Mary, Luke 1. xxviii. *Fagino anftaiaud ahafta,* " Rejoice, thou full of " grace;" correfponding exactly to the Gr. χαιρε; Ifl. *fognudur,* joy.

VER. 6. *Minny*—mother. This word belongs to the Infantine Lexicon, being ufed by very young children to their mothers. The prim. is *min,* little, beautiful, pleafant. Hence Goth. *minna,* to love; Alamm. *minnon;* Fr. *mignon,* and *mignard.* From hence *mama;* Scot. *mamy;* Fr. *maman;* Goth. *mamma;* " *vox*" (fays Ihre) " *qua blandientes in-* " *fantes matrem compellant.*" Welch *mam;* Armor. *mammaeth,* a nurfe. Gr. Μαμμα. Avia. Helladius (apud Phot. in Bibl.) informs us, that in ancient Greece the mothers were called παππαι. Confer Cange in Glofl. Græc. who alfo obferves that, in the middle Latinity, the *pap* was called *mamma;* and hence comes Fr. *mammelle.* Pelletier, in Lexi-

What thir flee twa togidder war fayen,
Whan wooing they war fae thrang.

III.

And O! quo' he, ann zee war as black,
As evir the crown o' your daddy's hat,

'Tis

co Brit. p. 570, juftly obferves, "*Ce mot eft peutetre* un des
" plus anciens du monde, car c'eft apres les cris, la premiere
" ouverture de la bouche du petit enfant, a qui la nature dicte,
" qu'il a befoin de nourriture, qu'il ne peut recevoir que de
" la *mammelle*, de celle qui lui a donne la vie." The Hebr.
em fignifies *mother*. From the Prim. *min*, little, is formed
the Lat. *minor*, (the *or* being the mark of comparifon), and
minimus. When we come to the Eighth Stanza of this Ballad,
we fhall explain the connection betwixt this and *winfome*.

VER. 2. *Wooing*.—A. S. *wogere*, lover, whence our *wooer*. It has been thought, and with probability, that this word
was formed from the cooing of the dove, as Douglas fays, p.
404. 27.

I mene our awin native bird, gentil Dow,
Singand on hir kynde, *I come hidder to woo*,
So prikking her grene curage for to crowde
In amorus voce, and *wowar* foundis lowde.

This is, at leaft, a better conjecture than that of Junius,
who deduces it from *woe*. The A. S. *wogan*, fign. to
marry.

STANZA III.

VER. 2. *Daddy*.—Engl. *dad*, father. The prim. is *da*,
di, every thing elevated in dignity and power, and being

denote

formed by a strong pressure of the tongue against the teeth, it comes to be a part of the child's first language, addressing him whom he is taught to look up to with reverence. Hence this radical word has given rise, in every language, to those which denote *elevation*. Such is the Celtic *Di*, God, the Supreme Being; *dun*, a hill; *dome*, *dum*, *din*, a judge. Hence too the Gr. Δυνασις, δυναμις, power; and the Lat. *dominus*, *dominatio*; the Greek δαμαω, to tame, *i. e.* bring into subjection; our *dame*, mistress.

In many dialects the *d* is changed into *t*, and most often, in those spoken in the North, though we also find it in the West, as in the Lat. *totus*, totality; Fr. *tasser*, *entasser*, to heap up. *Ta, tata*, father. From the idea of fatherly protection, were formed *di, ti*, prince or protector; and the Lat. *tego, tectum*, whence the Engl. *protect*, pro-tec-tion; and many more.

We shall here collect a few more infantine words, plainly derived from the structure of the vocal organs, and the most easy movements of their several parts. Such are, *pappa, mamma, dad, atta*; Fr. *bon; bobo, bibbi, puppet*; Fr. *poupee; bufs*. Thus Cato, de Lib. Educand. talking of this part of language, "cum "cibum et potum, *buas* et *papas*, vocent; matremq; *maman*, " patrem, *papam*." We may add to these, *pap, baba*, and even the ancient story of the word *bek*, pronounced by two children educated by Psammytichus king of Egypt, remote from all commerce with mankind, as Herodotus informs us. Confer. President de Brosse's Mechanism du Language, tom. 1. p. 231. seqq. To evince the universality of this truth, we might cite the Hebr. *phe*, and Chald. *phum*, mouth. Whence the *fari* of the Latins; the Hebr. *phar*, or *par*, ornament. Whence Latin *paro*, and Fr. *parer, parure*; Hebr. *pulful*, herbage. Whence the Lat. *puls*; the Gr. ζοω, and ζοσκω, to feed; ζοπα, meat; Lat. *voro, devoro*, and our *devour*;

E   ζαιο̣ι̣,

'Tis I wad lay thee be me bak,
And awa wi' thee I'd gang.

And

Caios, little; and the Ital. *bambino*; the Hebr. *bag*, nourishment, from the Prim. *bek*; from which is derived the Teuton. and Ger. *becken*, a baker; Babble, Ger. *babbelen*.

But how happen all these coincidencies? To this vain question we will only answer, in the words of the learned President last quoted, " L' homme parle, parceque Dieu l'a " creé etre *parlant*." The vocal organs are conſtructed alike in every tribe of mankind, and all children pronounce those ſounds firſt, which are moſt eaſily formed by the motions of theſe wonderful inſtruments. The ſounds they vary, and multiply, in proportion as practice makes them better acquainted with the organic powers, and more ready in the application of them. For the ſame reaſon, too, we find all the radical words in every tongue we are acquainted with, to be *monoſyllables*, theſe being the firſt eſſays of man in uſing the vocal organs.

To the liſt of languages, in which *dad*, *tat*, ſignifies *father*, let us add the Gael. *daid*; Welch *dad*; Corniſh *tad*; and Armorick *tat*.

Verſe 4. *Awa*] Engl. away; A. S. *an wæge*, from *wæg*, a way. Douglaſs, p. 124. l. 4.

" And the ſelf hour mycht haif tane us *awa*."

Gang] From *gae*, to *go*. This is an inſtance where our ſouthern neighbours have vitiated the true old pronounciation. The primitive letter G, being a guttural, is therefore painted in all the ancient alphabets like the neck of a camel, or with a remarkable *bending* in its figure, as in the Gr. Γ; the
Hebr.

THE GABERLUNZIE-MAN.

Hebr. ג. Hence it neceſſarily denotes every thing in the form of *canal* or *throat*, and every thing that runs or paſſes ſwiftly. We hope to produce many examples of this in our Scoto-Gothic Gloſſary. Mean while, we only obſerve the likeneſs in the following inſtances. Ulphila ſays *gaggan*, to go; and *gagg*, a ſtreet or road. Though this word occurs very often in the Codex Argenteus; yet Junius has omitted it in his learned gloſſary on Ulphila's verſion of the Goſpels. Ger. *gechen*; Belg. *gaen*; Dan. *gaa*. From hence comes the Lat. *eo*, without the *G*; and the Gr. *κ-ιειν*. Plato (in Cratylo, P. 281, *Fic.*) owns that *κ-ιεν* is a barbaric term. The other correſponding word ἐω, is undoubtedly Celtic; and here Voſſius (in *eo*) ſtops, being quite ignorant of the primitive word, and that no true radical term has ever more than one ſyllable. Ihre's deep reſearches into ancient languages enabled him to diſcover this truth; " Lingua" (ſays he, Gloſs. Vol. I. Col. 646.) " quo antiquior, eo monoſyllabicarum vocum ditior " eſt." Pity this very ingenious Etymologiſt had not carried this obſervation more into practice. The Armor. for *ga*, ſay *kea*, *ker*. The Goths call rogation days, *gandagar*; literally, *walking days*, from the proceſſions that then were uſually made round the corn-fields, during the darkneſs of popery. Ihre juſtly terms theſe *ambarvalia chriſtiana*. Rolf, the firſt who led the Scandinavians into Normandy, being a man of great ſtature, could find no horſe ſtrong enough to carry him. Being therefore always obliged to march on foot, from that circumſtance he was ſurnamed *Ganga Hrolf*, by the Iſlandic hiſtorians. *Gangare*, in the old Gothic laws, is " equus tolu-" tarius qui tolutim incedit." In one of the reſcripts of King Magnus, *anno*. 1345, the bridegroom ſends to his future ſpouſe, *en gangare ſadul, betzil, armakapo, och hata*, a horſe, ſaddle, bridle, cloak, and head-dreſs. Money of allowed currency is called *gangſe*; and *gangjarn*, hinges; and hence the

And O! quo' ſho, ann I war as whyte
As er the ſnaw lay on the dyke,

I'd

the Fr. *gond*. Perhaps our old word *ganze*, in Douglaſs, a *dart*, or *arrow*, comes from the Prim. *ga*, p. 461. 48.

" So thyk the *ganzies* and the flanys flew."

And p. 343. 46.

" Als ſwift as *ganze* or fedderit arrow fleis."

VER. 6. *Snaw*] Snow; another inſtance of the Engliſh perverſion of our ancient language. Ulph. *ſnaiws*; A. S. *ſnaw*; Allam. *ſne*; Iſl. *ſnior*; Swed. *ſnio*; Prim. *aw*; water, ever ſoft and flowing gently. Hence Gr. ναυειν; Heſich. ναυει, ῥεει, ϛρυσει, fluit, manat; A. S. *ſniwan*, to ſnow. How ridiculous are Junius, and the other lexicographers, who deduce our word from the Greek? Surely our anceſtors had ſeen ſnow long before they ſaw Greece. The ancient Goths were fond of prefixing *ſ* to many of their words; and hence the Prim. *aw*, water, became with them *ſnaw*; Sclavon. *ſneg*; Pol. *ſnieg*. When the *ſ* is taken away, it became *niv* with the Latins, and *neve* with the Italians; ſo the Gr. νιφας, denotes a thick falling ſnow.

Dyke] This has been prepoſterouſly derived from τειχος, a wall. The true primitive is the Celtic *digh*, ſolid, ſtrong, powerful; applied particularly to every rampart, whether to keep off enemies, beaſts, or inundations. Hence the τειχος of the Greeks; Ger. *teich*; Belg. *dyke*; French *digue*; the Ger. *dick*, ſolid; whence our word *thick*. The other German word *dight*, ſign. ſolid, connected; A. S. *dic*, rampart; *dician*, *gedician*, to build a rampart. Hence our

ditch;

I'd cleid me braw and lady like,
And awa wi' thee Ild gang.

IV.

ditch; A. S. *diker*, a ditcher; the Gr. δικελλα, a spade; δικελλιτης, a digger, one who uses the spade.

VER. 7. *Cleid*] Engl. *clothe*. Our *claith* is the true pronounciation, not the English *cloath*, our word being immediately formed from the Goth. *klaede*, clothing, and *klaeda*, to *clothe*. Prim. *kla—kle*, covering; A. S. *clath*. Observe, that the ancient Scandinavians said, *Eff par klæder*, a pair of garments, for a complete suit of clothes; the one formed the breeches, and the *troja*, or vest, the other. The old Teutonic Version of the Gospels (app. Ihre, vol. 1. col. 1076.) Luke xv. ver. 22. " Hemtin mik fram thet basta *par klæder* jak " hafwer;" Bring forth a pair of the best garments I have. Chron. Ryth. p. 121. " Eff hofweligt ors, ok *klæder* ett " par;" An excellent horse, and a pair of garments.

The Islanders pronounce it *klæde*; the Germans *kleide*, arm; *arm klade*, a scarf worn on the arm; *jaga klader*, a monk's gown.

Braw] Handsomely, elegantly. Prim. Celt. *bra*, strength, might, elegance; every thing having these qualities. Goth. *braf*, honest; Scot. *bravery*, sumptuous apparel. In the Bas—Bret. *braw*, arm, id. Hence the Fr. and our *brave*; Ital. *bravo*. Hence too the Goth. *brage*, a hero, and *Brage*, the name of one of the companions of Odid, of whom *Edda, Agietus ad Spæki*, &c. He was very elegant, and wise, and a great poet; so that from him all persons, both men and women, who excelled in these arts, were called *Bragmadur*. From the same source the *bragebækare*, or large cup, drunk off by the new King, just before he a-
scended

IV.

Between the twa was made a plot,
They raife a wee befor the cock,
                                        And

fcended the throne, while he folemnly vowed to atchieve fome great deed in arms, of which many inftances occur in Snorro, and the other hiftorians of the North. This ceremony gave rife to the ufage, according to which the knights, in ancient times, made vows of the fame kind at their folemn banquets. The learned and accurate Annalift, to whom Scotland owes the elucidation of many hiftorical difficulties, obferves (ad an. 1306) that Edward made a vow after this form, by which he bound himfelf to punifh Robert Bruce.—See alfo St Palaye Mem. De l'ancienne cheval. tom. 1. p. 184, and 244.

STANZA IV.

VER. 1. *Twa*] Ger. *twee*; A. S. *twa*; Welch *dau*, *dwy*; Armor. *du*; Cimber. *tu*; Sued. *twa*; Celt. id. Whence Gr. *δυο*, and Lat. *duo*. Hence our *twin*; Dan. *twilninger*; Alam. *zuinlinge*; A. S. *getwinn*. Douglas calls fheep of two years old *twinleris*, p. 130, v. 34.

" Fyfe twinleris Britnyt he, as was the gyis."

Coufer page 202, ver. 16. as being two *winters*, i. e. two years old; Ulphila *twai*, two. Hence to *twinne*, ufed both in
                                                    Scotland

And wylily they fhot the lock,
And faft to the bent ar they gane.

Up-
Scotland and England to fignify, to feparate, divide into two parts. Chaucer, l. 518.

" The life out of her body for to twyne."

Pard. Prol. 167:

———" He muft ytwin
" Out of that place."———

VER. 2. *Wee*] Little. This is an infantine word, denoting every thing *little*. Ger. *wenig*. Hence our *wean*, i. e. *wee-ane*, a little child. Of the fame family, as I conjecture, is the word *weaena*, which the learned Lord Hailes fhewed me in an Englifh book, where it denoted a *fimpleton*, or unlearned man; little of underftanding, as the Dutch ftill fay, *Klein van verftanda*.

VER. 3. *Wylily*] Cunningly. A. S. *wile*, whence our *guile*, the *W* being often changed for *G*. Belg. *gylen*, and in the Lower Germany they fay *begigeln*, to beguile. Dan. *adwilla*, to deceive. Ifl. *viel*, deception; hence *Willurunnur*, Runæ deceptrices. Sax. Chron. ad an. 1128, *Thurh his micele wiles*, " Through his many *wiles*, or tricks." In a church-yard in Scotland are the following lines on the tombftone of a Magiftrate:

" He was baith wyss and *wyly*,
" For which the town made him a bailey."

Under-

Upon the morn the auld wyf raife,
And at her leifure pat on her claife,
Syne to the fervants bed fcho gaes,
  To fpeir for the filly poor man.

V.

Under-waiftcoat is by Douglas called the *wylie-coat*, p. 201, v. 40.

" In doubill garment cled, and *wyle-cot*."

As this inner-veft (fays Ruddiman) cunningly, or hiddenly, keeps us warm.

VER. 4. *Bent*] Properly a marfhy place, producing the coarfe grafs called *bent*, from its fmall limber ftalk eafily *bent*, fays Minfhew; but may it not be rather derived from *ben*, a hill, as this coarfe grafs is common on the fides of hills, and on the rifing ground on the fea-fhore, or fandy hillocks, in Scotland? In Gaelic *ban* fignifies wild or wafte ground, on which this fpecies of grafs is generally found.

VER. 6. *Claife*] Vide Note to Stanza III. Ver. 7.

VER. 7. *Syne*] Afterwards, then. Douglas writes *fen*, p. 100, v. 1.

" *Sen* the deceis of my forry hufband."

Senfyne, fince that time, id. p. 44, v. 26.

—" *Senfyne* has ever mair
" Backwart of grekis the hope went."

Teuton. G. *fyn* and *findes*, whence our *fince*. Alam. *ejnzen*; and *Otfrid*, Lib. 3. cap. 26. *findes*.

Joh tharbetin thes *findes*,
Their heiminges.
                                                    " And

" And were deprived of their country *from that time*." Ulphila, Luke 17. v. 4. *Sintham.* Ubi confer Jun. Suio-Goth. *naganſinn*, and more shortly *nanſin*; *nanſtin*, sometimes; *hwatſin*, how often; *ſinnam oh ſinnom*, by degrees, gradually. Whence the Lat. *ſenſim*, understood by none of their Lexicographers.

As particles in general form a difficult part of language, a philosophical enquiry into the origin of these might highly deserve the attention of the critic. It is thought that many of them, being *monoſyllables*, will be found to be *radical words*. Such are, Engl. *if*; Scot. *giff*; A. S. *gif, gyf*; Gr. *ει*, enlarged by composition to ειτεε, and ειτε; and many others might be named. To derive *if* from *giff*, as some have done, is ridiculous, and shews that some writers will rather adopt the most futile conjectures, than ingeniously confess their ignorance. The limits we have prescrib'd ourselves in these notes, do not permit us to enlarge on this at present.

VER. 8. *Speir*] Prim. is *pa—ſa*, the mouth. Hence *ſpeech*; Germ. *ſpuren*, to enquire. The learned and ingenious Mr Gebelin, to whom we confess ourselves indebted for the only rational principles of Etymology we have seen, in his *Monde Primitive*, tom. 5. p. 790, has shewn, that the P, in all the ancient alphabets, figures *the mouth opened*, viewed in profile; and, by necessary consequence, all the actions of that organ, as *ſpeaking, eating, drinking*, &c. And this position he has evinced to demonstration, by innumerable examples. We confine ourselves here to what regards the word *ſpeir*. We have already observed, that the general meaning relates to *ſpeech*; Lat. *ſari*; Fr. *pa-rler, ſa-ribole*, vain and idle talking. Afterwards it was used in the North for *wiſdom, prudence*. Hence Isl. *ſpakr*, a wise man; in Goth. *ſpak*, the same; *ſpakum bonda*, a prudent man; Isl. *ſpakmæle*, the sayings of the wise; Alam. *ſpaker*, and *ſpeke*, wisdom.

F Tatian,

V.

She gaed to the bed whar the beggar lay,
The ftrae was cauld, he was away;

She

Tatian, cap. 12. *Folfpahida*, full of wifdom. Ifl. *fpeja*, to fpeculate, or confider. In reftricting the general meaning, it came to fignify only, to *divine*, *prophecy*. Ifl. *fpa*, to prophecy; whence our *fpae*, to foretell future events. From this the Latins have formed *fpecio*, *aufpex*, *arufpex*, and the like. Douglas, p. 101. 50:

"O welaway, of *fpaimen* and divines
"The blind myndis."——

And p. 80. 26:

——"The harpie Celeno
"*Spais* unto us an fereful takin of wo."

The *Volufpa*, containing the theology of the Scandinavians, has its name from thence, and literally fignifies a poem artfully contrived, *or with much wifdom*, compounded of *wola*, *wool*, art, and *fpa*, poem or fpeech. Hence Ifl. *wolundr*, artificer; and *wolundurhus*, a labyrinth.

STANZA V.

VER. 2. *Strae*] Engl. *ftraw*; A. S. *ftreow*, *ftrew*; Al. *kiftreiew*, to ftraw; Mæfo-Goth. *ftrawan*; A. S. *ftreawian*. The chamber *furn:fhed* in Mark xiv. 15. is called in Gr. εςτρωμενον, and by Ulphila *gaftrawith*. The ancients not

only

Scho clapt her hands, cry'd, dulefu-day!
For some o' our gier will be gane.
Sume

only filled their beds with straw, but on solemn days the floors were covered with it; and we remember to have read, that Queen Elizabeth's state-rooms were strawed with green grafs or hay. It was also a part of the holding of several manors, both in England and Scotland, to furnish straw for the Royal apartments, when the King made a progress. In the Scandinavian writings, the straw used at the festival of *Yule*, was called *Iulhalm*, vide Ihre in V. So in Olaf's *Trygwas*. Saga, p. 1. p. 204. it is said of Thorleif, *Seeft han nither utarliga utarsiga i halmin*, He sat down on the furthest part of the straw. Snorro tells us, tom. 1. p. 403. that when Olaf, son of Harald, came to see his mother, *Tweir karlar, baro halmin i golfid*, Two servants brought straw into the apartments; and, in the History of Alf, p. 41. one of the Princes in the Court of King Hior, *Their voru i halminum nidur a golfinu*, They sat on the ground on the straw. It would appear, that this was commonly done in winter; for the same reason we use carpets to keep the feet warm: For it is remarked of Olaf Kyrra, that he had his apartments covered with straw, winter and summer; *han let giora stragolff um vetur, sem um sumur*. The same mode was observed in France. In a charter of the year 1271 (ap. Cange in *Jonchare*) " Item debet et tenetur dictus Raulinus pro prædictis, Jon- " chare domum D. Episcopi quando necesse est." Vide id. in *Junkus*. Confer Spelm. in *Straftura*.

VER. 4. *Gier*, or *gear*] Clothes, furniture, riches. To what has been said in the preface of this word, and in the notes to Stan. 4. ver. 5. we have little to add. The prim. is

F 2

Ge;

Sume ran to coffers, and fume to kifts,
But nought was ftown that cou'd be mift;
                                    She

Ge; Gr. γη, the *earth*; fource of all our riches. Hence ufed by the Scots indifcriminately, to fignify every thing we value, goods, tools, apparel, armour. So Douglafs fays, *graithed in his gear*, armed at all points. *Gear*, in fome of our old poets, is ufed for the *membra viri genitalia*. A. S. *gyrian*, to clothe. Cædmon, 23. 7. *gyred wædum*, put on his weeds or garments.

VER. 5. *Kifts*] Engl. chefts. The primitive of this is found in the form of the letter *c*, (for which the northern dialects generally ufe the *k*) fignifying every hollow, like the hollow of the hand; as *cavus, cavea*; Gr. κοιλος; *cavity, cave*, &c. This obtains in every language, as we fhall prove at fome length in our Scoto-Gothic Gloffary. With refpect to this word, we formed it from Goth. *kifta*, a cheft; whence *kiftafæ*, precious goods which are kept in kifts; Ifl. *kiftu*; Welch *cift, cyft*; Ger. *kaften*; Fr. *caiffe*; Gr. κιςτη; Lat. *cifta*, the origin of which fimple word is not to be found in the many Greek and Latin Dictionaries we have. Hence too *cifterna*, our ciftern. The etymon of this word by Feftus is too curious to be omitted; *cifterna dicta eft, quod cis ineft infra terram*. Such are the reveries produced by ignorance of firft principles. We add further, that the Perfians call a *cheft*, or *kift, caftr*. In the north it fignifies a prifon where thieves are confined; *teif kifta*. The Latins ufed a fimilar phrafe, *In arcam conjici*, vid. Cic. pro Milone, cap. 22. The Iflanders call a coffin *leikiftu*, as we alfo do, and the Anglo-Saxons. Luke 7. 14. *Iha cyfte æthran*, He touched the coffin.

VER

She dancid her lane, cry'd, Praife be bleft!
I have ludg'd a leil poor man.

VI.

VER. 6. *Stown*] Engl. *ftolen* ; Prim. *ftill*, tacitly, hiddenly; Goth. *ftilan*; A. S. *ftelan*; Swed. *ftiala*, to fteal; Tueton. *ftille*, quiet, fecret. Hence our Scots *ftowth*, ftealing, which we find applied to amorous pleafures, as being fecret, by Douglafs, p. 402. 52.

" Hys mery *ftowth*, and paftyme lait ziftrene."

So the Latins, *Veneris furta*. *Stiala* is ufed by the Northerns in the fame fenfe as we fay, to *fteal away* ; fo *ftiala fig bort* ; and *komma ftialandes uppa en*, to come privately upon one. They alfo ufe it to denote *hiding*, concealing, the meaning of the primitive. Hift. Alex. M. Apud Ihre, v. 2. 267.

Jordan kan eij gullit fwa ftiala.
The earth cannot fo hide the gold.

Ulphila's *bliftus* fignifies a *thief*, from *bliftan*, to hide. Hence our Scots *to lift*, to fteal. From the primitive *ftill* is the Gr. ϛηλαϛθηι, to hide; and the Lat. *celo*, the *ft* being often added in the Scythian words; as *ftrafwa*, for *rofwa*, *fpoliare* ; *ftræcha*, for *ræcka*, *tendere*, &c. The Iflandic *ftiarlare* is a *thief*, a *ftealer;* and hence the Latin *ftellio*, *ftellionatus*, *ftollatura*, occult fraud, as the ingenious Ihre has juftly obferved, and thereby unfolded the true etymon, about which all the Latin Lexicographers were puzzled.

VER. 7. *Praife be bleft*] God be praifed. This is a common form ftill in Scotland with fuch as, from reverence, decline to ufe the facred name.

VI.

Since nathing's awa, as we can learn,
The kirn's to kirn, and milk to carn,

Gae

VER. 8. *Leil*] Loyal, honest, truly. Dougl. p. 86. 46.

"The *ceremonies leil*, i. e. holy ceremonies."

And p. 43. 20.

"——by the faith unfylit, and the *lele* lawte."

STANZA VI.

VER. 1. *Awa*] Engl. *away*. Angl. Sax. *an wæge*, from *wæg*, a way. Dougl. p. 124. 4.

"And the felf hour mycht haif tane us *awa*."

VER. 2. *Kirn*] Churn. This is the fame with the Ger. and Scot. *quern*, a hand-mill for grinding corn, butter being produced by the continued action of turning round. In the A. S. *quearn*, or *cwyrn*; Dan. *handquern*, hand-mill. The prim. is *gur, kyr*, any thing circular; Arab. *kur*, a round tower; *ma-kur*, a turban; Hebr. *gur*, to affemble; and *ha-gur*, a belt; Ifland. *gyrta*; whence our *girth*, and the verb to *gird*. Hence too Gr. γυρ-ος; Lat. *gyrus*, and *girare*. The Fr. *ceinture*, and our *girdle* are from the fame root, and the Gaelic *cor*, whence *cord*; Ger. *gurt*, a belt; and *gurten*, to gird about; Welch *gwyr*, bent; Bas. Bret. *gourifa*, to begird; Bafq. *gur*, around; *girata*, to roll about; *gurcilla*, chariot wheel; *guiroa*, the feafons, *i. e.* the revolutions of the heavens. The Gr. κυρτος, *vaulted*, and κιρκος, *round*, have the fame origin; alfo ἀγορα, a place of public affembly where

the

Gae butt the houfe, lafs, and waken my bairn,
And bid her come quickly ben.
The

the people ftood round the orators. In Varro we find the ancient Latin *guro*, to make round; and the common words,
circus, circulus, circum, circuitus, and many more, all deduced from the fame root. The *gier-falcon* has its name from
the circular flight he makes; and the Ger. *kurbis*, a gourd;
and the Lat. *cu-cur-bita*, cucumber; Gr. ςπυγος, a quiver.
It were eafy to add ten times this number of words, all taking
their origin from *gyr*; but we only further mention *gir*,
the Scots name for the *hoop* the boys drive before them with
a rod along the ftreets.

Our pronounciation of this word *kirn*, is more correct than
that of the Englifh; for the Gothic verb is *kernais*, to *churn*;
Fenn. *kirnun*; and the churn itfelf is called in Efthonia *kir-
nu*, and in Iceland *kernuafk*. The round Tower of Stock-
holm is called *Keerna* by the ancient writers, as the learned
Ihre informs us (Gloff. vol. 2. p. 1057.) to which we only
add, that the Gr. κιρναω *mifceo*, has the fame origin, though
it has not been obferved by Junius, or any other.

VER. 2. *Earn*] To thicken or curdle milk. Ger. *gerin-
nan*, to coagulate. The root is only found in the Armorick,
in which language *go* fign. fermentation; *goi*, to .ferment.
Hence the Goth. *gora*, effervefcere; *drinkat gores*, the ale
ferments, or works; Ger. *gærung*, effervefcence; and the
Swed. *gorning*, whence our *earning*, rennet.

VER. 3. *Butt*] From Belg. *buyten*, without; oppofed to
binnen, within. Thus Douglas ufes it, p. 123. 40.

" In furious flambe kendlit, and birnand fchire,
" Spredant fra thak to thak, baith *butt* and ben."
The

The primitive is found in the Goth *bur-ho,* habitation; Ancient Goth. *bua-bu,* to inhabit; whence *bur,* and Ifl. *byr* and *bycht,* habitation. A. S. *bur,* a chamber; and Ray fays, that in the North of England it is ftill pronounced *boor,* and *bor.* Swed. *burtont,* floor of the houfe; *iungfrubur,* apartment where the daughters of the family fleep; βυριον, οικημα, habitation. From the Goth. *byr,* we form *byre,* a cow-houfe. This primitive is alfo found in the Hebr. *beth,* and Perf. *bat,* a houfe; Teuton. *bod,* whence the Engl. *abode;* Gael. *bwth, bottega,* a fhop; Fr. *boutigue.* That part of Edinburgh where the merchants have their fhops, is called *Luckenbooths,* rather *Lockenboths,* from the booths, or fhops, being locked up at night.

VER. 3. *Waken*] To a-wake. Prim. *wak, watch.* Hence Ulph. *vakan,* to awaken; *vaknandans,* vigilantes. All the Nothern dialects ufe this word. Goth. and Ifl. *waka;* Ger. *watchten;* Alam. *uuachan.* The Goths fay alfo *wakna,* to watch; Ifl. *wekia, watch,* and Goth. *waht,* id. Ulphila fays, *wahtus;* Alam. *uuaht;* B. Lat. *wacta,* cap. 3. an. 813. c. 34. " Si quis wactam aut wardam demiferit." Vide Cange in *Wacta.* Hence in our old Scots Laws, to *watch and ward,* duty of citizens to defend their town, and for which they often obtained fingular privileges from the Crown. *Wactar,* a watchman: It fignifies alfo to *beware; Wacta fig for en,* to be upon one's guard. From this, too, come the Lat. *vigilo, vigilium;* the Fr. *guetter,* and *garder,* our *guard.* The waiting a dead body before interment, is called in Sued. *wahftuga.* Hence our phrafe *to wake a corpfe,* and *leikwake,* compounded of the two words Goth. *leik,* a dead body, and *wakna,* to watch.

Bairn] Child. Prim. Gael. *bar;* A. S. *bearn;* Alam. *barn.* Hence comes Gaelic *beirn,* and Goth. *baera,* both fignifying *to bear.* We find our primitive in the Hebr. *Bar,*

Creator,

The fervant gaed quhar the dochter lay,
The fheits war cauld, fcho was away,
And

Creator, and *Bara*, creare. In the fragment of Sanchoniathon, *Beruth*, or *Berut*, is called the fpoufe of *El-ion*, or the Moft High, becaufe God alone creates; and hence allegorically *Creation* is called the *fpoufe of God*. In the Syriac, *bar* fignifies a fon. We fay *bairn-team*, brood of children, from the Saxon *team*, progeny; hence a *teeming-woman*. In our old poets, *bairn* is often ufed to fignify a full-grown man. So Douglas, p. 244. 33.

" Cum furth quhat e'er thou be, *berne bald*."

And elfewhere:

————" And that awfull *berne*,
" Berying fchaftis fedderit with plumes of the erne."

The fame author ufes *barnage* for an army, or troop of warriors; but Mr Ruddiman was far miftaken in deriving it from the Lat. *baro*. We find the ancient Englifh poets ufed *child* in the fame fenfe. See the ballad of the *Child of Elle*, in Percy's Collection, vol. 1. page 107.

" And yonder lives the *childe* of Elle,
" A young and comely knight."

Vide ibid. p. 44. where two knights are called *children*.

VER. 4. *Ben*] The oppofite of *butt*, in the former verfe, fignifying the inner-part of the houfe. From the Dutch *binnen*, within, oppofed to *buyten*, without; A. S. *buta* and *binnen*, butt and ben.

VER. 5. *Gaed*] Vide Note to Stanza I. Ver. 6.

G *Dochter*]

And faſt to her gudewife 'gan ſay,
Scho'ṣ aff wi' the Gaberlunzie-man,

VII.

O fy gar ride, and fy gar rin,
And haſte ye find theſe traiters agen :

For

Dochter] Engl. *daughter;* Ulph. *dauhtar.* We here obſerve how cloſely our ſpelling agrees with the Anglo-Saxon, in which it is wrote *dohter*, *dohtor*, and *dohtur;* Alam. *dohtor*, *dohter*, and *thohter;* Belg. *dochter.* The Gr. Θυγατηρ has a manifeſt affinity to all theſe.

Ver. 6. *Cauld*] Another inſtance of our care in following the original orthography. Ulphila writes, *calds;* A. S. *ceald;* Iſl. *kaldur* and *kulde;* Alam. *kalt;* Dan. *kuld;* all ſignifying *cold.*

Ver. 7. *Faſt*] Quick or ſwift. Prim. Welch *fleſt*, agile, haſty. This is a quite different word from the Engliſh *faſt*, fixed or ſtable, which comes from the Mæſo-Gothic *faſtan*, to keep or hold faſt.

'Gan] For *gan*, *began;* and thus Douglas elſewhere uſes it, as well as our more ancient poets.

Ver. 8. *Aff*] Off; but all the other Northern dialects write this word with an *a*. Ulph. *af;* Dan. *aff;* Belg. *af:* The Lat. *ab*, and the Gr. ὐπι, are quite ſimilar, eſpecially when we obſerve that the Greek word, before another beginning with an aſpirate, is written ἀφ.

STANZA VII.

Ver. 1. *Fy*] Fy upon. Prim. Welch *fy*, and *hei*, whence *hiadd*, abominable; Iſl. *fue*, rottenneſs; Belg. *foey;*

hence

THE GABERLUNZIE-MAN. 51

hence the Lat. *vah*, Ital. *vah*, Fr. *fi*. The Gr. φευ is by the Grammarians called φωνη χ·τλ ασικη, Vox ejus qui fe indigna pati conqueritur. In old Englifh this particle always denotes *averfion*. Chaucer, La. Prol. v. 80.

" Of fuch curfed ftories I fay *fie*."

And N. P. T. v. 73.

" *Fie* ftinking fwine! *fie* foul mote the befall."

From hence the Scots formed *Fyle*, to foul; and the Engl. *Defile*. We alfo fay *Fych*, on feeling a bad fmell, or feeing any dirty object, from the Celt. *cach*, *kakoa*, and *caffo*, ftinking. Hence our *kakie*, ventrem exonerare. From this origin, too, comes the old French appellation *cagots*, *cacous*, *cakets*, given to lepers, who being confidered as abominable, were fhut out from all fociety in the middle ages. Thefe miferable wretches were found in great numbers about the 12th and 14th centuries, fpread over Gafcony, Bearn, and the two Navarres, on both fides the Pyrenean mountains. Thefe were not allowed to traffick with their fellow citizens; had a feparate door to enter into the churches, and a holy water-font, which they only ufed; were forbid the ufe of arms; nay, fuch was the univerfal horror of mankind againft them, that the States of Berne, anno 1460, applied for an order to prohibit their walking the ftreets bare-footed, left others might catch the infection, and to oblige them to wear on their garments the figure of a goofe's foot, which, it would appear, they had neglected to do for many years paft. In the ancient *For. de Navarre*, compiled about the year 1074, we fee them called *Gaffos* and *Gakets* at Bourdeaux. We find, among the Laws of the Dukes of Brittany, anno 1474 and 1475, orders given, that none of the *Cacofi-caquets*, or *Cacos*, should appear without a bit of red cloth sewed on the outer-garment. They were forbid even to cultivate any land but their gardens, and were confined to the single trade of carpenters. Bullet (*Diction. Celt.*) gives the following account of the rise of the public hatred against these poor people: " Cacous (says he) Nom que les Bas Brettons donnent par injure aux Cordiers et aux Tonneliers, contre lesquelles le menu peuple est si prevenu, qu'ils ont besoign de l'autorité du Parlement de Bretagne pour avoir le sepulture, et la liberté de faire les fonctions du Christianisme avec les autres, parce qu'ils sont crus sans raison, descendre des Juifs disperses apres la ruine de Jerusalem, et qu'ils passent pour lepreux de race.—Les *Cacous* sont nommés *cacqueux* dans un arret du Parlement du Bretagne." Here we have a people, living in the most deplorable state of slavery, from age to age, like the Gibeonites subjected to the Jews, and treated in the same manner as the Gauls were, after being conquered by the ancient *Franks* of Germany; the very name they went by, implying the most rooted aversion, though nobody ever gave any account of the reason of this appellation; for the frivolous dissertations of *Marca* and *Venuti* leave us quite in the dark as to this, as well as to the causes of this extraordinary hatred against a devoted race from age to age. We therefore adopt the account of it given by the learned and most ingenious *Gebelin*, (Monde Primitif, tom. 5. p. 247) that they were the scattered remains of the original inhabitants of Gascony and Lower Brittany, who, being conquered by those now called *Bretons*, and the Cantabri, who invaded Brittany and Berne, were reduced to this miserable state by their Lords, in order to leave them no means of revolt, and to render them useful as slaves. Du Cange informs us, that the celebrated Hevin first obtained, from the Parliament of Rennes, a repeal of those cruel and ridiculous constitutions

THE GABERLUNZIE-MAN. 53

conftitutions againft the *Cacous.* But the word *Cagot* ftill remains a term of reproach, and now fignifies a *hypocrite.* Had we leifure, it would be amufing to compare the miferable ftate of the poor *Cagots,* with that infamy which is entailed, in Hindoftan, on the caft or tribe of the *Sooders.* But we have already made this note too long ; and all the apology we can offer is, that we flatter ourfelves the reader will be glad to find here an account of a fet of men, whofe very name is little, if at all, known in this Ifland, and againft whom far more intolerable feverities were exercifed, than by our anceftors againft the lepers, who abounded both in England and Scotland during the middle ages.

Gar] Force one to act, to conftrain. Prim. Celtic *gor, gar,* force, ftrength, elevation, abundance ; vide Dict. Celt. de Bullet in *Gorchaled,* and *Gor.* Hence Breton. *gor,* tumour, elevation ; Gaelic *gorm,* nobleman, grandee. In the language of Stiria and Carniola, mountain ; *gora,* in Sclavon. id. Polon. *gora-hegy,* a cape or promontory ; Lapland, and Finland, *kor-kin,* high ; Hebr. *gor,* to heap up ; Arab. *ghurur,* pride, ambition ; whence Gr. γαυρος, proud, elated ; Old French *gaur,* id. Celt. *gorain,* to cry out with vehemence, which greatly illuftrates the primitive fignification of our *gar ;* Welfh, *gorchfygiad,* to force or conftrain ; Suio-Goth. *gora,* antiq. *gara,* facere ; vide Ihre in *gora,* where this elegant etymologift has obferved the agreement betwixt this word and our *gar.* Adde Lye addit. Etymol. Junii ; but none of thefe writers have gone back to the Primitive Celtic ; Aremor. *gra,* facere. From this root, too, comes the Latin *gero,* applied fometimes to war, *gerere bellum* ; vide Livy, l. 39. c. 54. Ifl. *giora,* to act ; Alam. *garen, garuuen.* The reader may turn to our Introduction, where he will find fome other obfervations on this word, to which we only add, that *carve* comes from this root.

Ver.

For fcho's be burnt, and hee's be flean,
The weirifou' Gaberlunzie-man.
Some rade upo' horfe, fome ran a-fit,
The wife was wude, and out o' her wit;

Scho

VER. 3. *Scho's—Hee's*] She fhall—He fhall; a contraction frequently in the mouths of our country people.

VER. 4. *Weirifou*] *Fou* for *full*, it being cuftomary in Scots to change the *l* into *w*, as *roll, row; fcroll, fcrow; tolbooth, toubooth; pol, pow,* &c. Ruddiman. From *fou*, we form *fouth*, plenty, abundance. So Douglafs, p. 4. v. 6.

"That of thy copious fouth or plentitude."

Thus from *deep, depth; rew, reuth,* &c. This is alfo remarked by Mr Ruddiman, Gloff.

VER. 6. *Wude*] Mad. Ger. *wuth*, rage; A. S. *wod*, mad; Teut. *uueuten*, to be mad; A. S. *wedan*, id. Whence perhaps the Scandinavians called their Mars *Woden*. Doug. p. 16. 29.

"The ftorm up bullerit fand, as it war *wod.*"

And p. 423, 16.

"Wod wroith he worthis for difdene."

Dutch *woed*, fury; Ulphila, Mark v. 18. *wods*, poffeffed with a Devil; A. S. *wod*, mad; Ifl. *æde*, furor; Alam. *unatage*, furious. From this root the Gr. ουταν, vulnerare, pugnare; and οιδαινειν, to fwell with anger.

VER.

Scho cou'd na gang, nor yet cou'd fcho fit,
But ay fcho curs't and fcho bann'd.

VIII.

Mein tym far hind out o'wr the lee,
Fu' fnug in a glen whar nane cou'd fee,
                                    Thir

Ver. 7. *Gang*] Mæfo Goth. *gagga*, pronounced *ganga*; as in the Greek when two *gammas* follow each other. Vide ad Stan. I. v. 6.

Ver. 8. *Ban*] To curfe. Goth. *banna*, fign. fimply to forbid; *forbanna*, Divis devovere. The primitive Celt. *ban*, a *tie*; whence our *bond* and *band*. Hence marriage *banns*. The Ifl. *forbanna*, fign. to excommunicate or put out of fociety. Hence our *ban-ifh*, and the Ital. *bandito*, our *banditti*; *a-ban-don*, to give up our claim to any thing, to loofen our tie to it. The bond by which the king's vaffals are obliged to follow their fovereign to the field, is, in France, called the *ban*, and *arriere ban*. Thus to *bann* one, literally fign. to put him *under the bond of a curfe*. Hence Gael. *bana*, tied; Fr. *bande*, *bander*, our *band* or *company*, perfons linked together by one common tie, or bond; *bandage*, to bend; Fr. *ruban*, whence *ribbon*, literally, a fillet of a red colour. Hence, too, in the French, the barbarous *droit d'aubaine*, by which the lord of the foil inherited all that a ftranger died poffeffed of in his territory. We find, in the Bar. Lat. *albani*, and *aubani*, a ftranger; concerning which word many idle conjectures have been publifhed, as derived from *advena*, and *Albanus*, a Scotfman. But it is compofed of *al*, another, and *ban*, jurifdiction, literally a perfon living under *other laws*.

laws. The Ifl. *bann*, to curfe, is ftill ufed in the north of England.

STANZA VIII.

VER 1. *Hind*] This is the primitive of *behind, hindermoſt*; Scot. *hindmoſt*; and is found in all the ancient dialects of the north; Ulphila, *hindar, hindana*, back, after; *hindumiſts*, hindermoſt; A. S. *hindan*, behind. Hence comes the verb to *hinder*, to impede; Dan. *hindṛe, forhindra*; Belg. *hinderen, verhinderen*. From this root comes the A. S. *hinderling*, properly one who comes far behind his anceſtors, *familiæ ſuæ opprobrium*. In Ll. Edw. Confeſſ. c. 35. Occidentales Saxonici habent in proverbio fummi defpectus, *hinderling*; i. e. omni honeſtate dejecta et recedens imago; the fcandal of his family.

VER. 2. *Snug*] The primitive of feveral northern words, all fignifying *hiding, concealment*; Dan. *fniger*, fubterfugio; *fnican*, to crawl about hiddenly; whence Engl. *fneak*, a fneaking fellow. Lye was miſtaken in deriving it from Iſl. *fnoggur*, celer. The Gael. *fnaighim*, is the fame with the Saxon *fnican*; Dan. *fnige fig aff veyen*, to fneak away. The Scots *fnod*, neat, trim, may come alfo from this fource, as it is evidently the fame with the Gothic, *fnug*, ſhort and neat; *en fnug piga*, a neat girl; Iſl. *fnylld*, elegance. Ray fays, that in the north of England, they pronounce it *fnog*; *fnogly geard*, handfomely dreſſed.

Glen] Old Engliſh *glin*, or *glyn*; Gael. *gleann*. It denotes a large, level tract of ground, bounded on each fide by ridges of floping mountains. Hence we have in Scotland *Strathmore, Strathſpey, Strathern*. There is this difference between the Saxon *Dale*, and the Gaelic *Strath*. The former denotes a narrow valley, bounded on each fide by a

ridge

Thir twa, wi' kindly fport and glee,
Cut frae a new cheefe a whang.

The
ridge of fteep mountains, commonly with a river running through the middle; the latter anfwers the above defcription, which needs not to be repeated.

VER. 3. *Twa*] Ulphila *twai*; A. S. *twa*; Welfh *dau*, *dwy*; Gael. *do*; Swed. *twa*; Ifl. *tueir*. Hence the Gr. δυω, and *twain*; our Scot. *twin*, literally fign. to fplit into two parts, to feparate. It is alfo ufed by Chaucer in this fenfe, R. R. 5077.

" Trowe nat that I woll hem twinne."

And Troil, 4. 1197.

" There fhall no deth me fro' my ladie twinne."

From this root, too, is formed *twine*, thread, *i. e.* to double it; A. S. *twinen*; vide Exod. c. 39. 29. Sued. *twynna*; Dan. *tuinder*, to fpin; *tuinde trade*, twined thread; Belg. *tweyn draed*. In Teutonifta, *twern yarn*, *duinum tuinum*; A. S. *twinne*, to twihe.

Glee] Mirth, gladnefs; Ifl. *gled*, *gladde*, I have made glad; *mig gladur*, it is a pleafure to me; Sax. *glæd*, and our *glad*. With Chaucer *glee* denotes a concert of vocal and inftrumental mufic. Sir Top. R. v. 126.

" His merie men commanded he
" To maken him both game and glee."

Fa. Lib. 3. 161.

" There faw I fitt in other fees,
" Playing on other fundrie glees."

H

The A. S. Verſion of Paſtor. 26. 2. *David defeng his hearkan, and geſtilde his wodthraga mid tham gligge.* David took his harp, and ſtilled his madneſs with muſic. *Gligman,* mimus, ſcurra; *Gligmon,* id. Junius rightly conjectures, that *glig* was firſt uſed to denote inſtruments inflated by the breath, though afterwards indiſcriminately applied to every muſical ſound. This is confirmed by the Iſlandic *gliggur,* flatus, breath. A certain ſpecies of *catch* is ſtill called a *glee.* A. S. *gle,* joy, and without the *g* the Goth. *lek,* to laugh; we ſay *gaaff,* to laugh loudly, and with the open mouth. From the idea of joy, *gle* and *gla* came to ſignify every thing bright, ſplendid. Hence a multitude of words, Iſl. *glaumur,* joy; whence our old Scots *glamur,* often employed to ſignify *incantations,* becauſe, by ſuch arts, the mind was thought to be greatly moved, and to look on things indifferent as of great conſequence. Goth. *glans,* and Alam. *klanz,* ſplendour; whence our *glance,* from *gla,* light; *gloa,* to ſhine. From this laſt the Eng. *glow, glow-worm*; A. S. *glowan,* to glow; Swed. *glod;* Gael. *glo;* A. S. *gled;* Ger. *glut;* all ſignifying a *live coal.* Iſl. *glia;* Friſl. *glian,* to ſhine; Sax. *gleij,* ſplendidus; and hence the Gr. αιγλη, ſplendour; which none of our Lexicographers have been able to explain. Hence, too, Engl. *glitter,* by Ulphila written *glitmunjan;* Iſl. *glitta;* Ger. *gleiſſen;* Swed. *gliſtra, gniſta;* Sax. *glinſtern,* and the Gr. αγλαιζεϑαι; Iſl. *gliſt,* and *glaſt,* nitidus. So Snorro, v. 1. *Glaſt med gulli, och ſilfri,* ſhining with gold and ſilver. Gr. γελειν, ſplendere; and Heſychius explains γελας, αυγην ηλιε, a ſun-beam; αγλαος, ſplendidus; γλαυςςω, ſplendeo; γλαυκος, γλαυρος, ſplendidus; Goth. *glaſſa,* and our *glaze;* Iſl. *glas,* our *glaſs.* We call the ſlipperymucus, growing on ſtones in the river, *glitt*; and *glatt* in Gothic is nitidus, lævis. Hence Engl. *gloſs;* Goth. *gles,* Succinum. Vide Tacit. Mor. Ger. cap. 45. Plin. H. N. lib. 26. c. 3.

From

THE GABERLUNZIE-MAN. 59

From the fame root are derived Goth. *glimra, glindra*, to shine, whence our *glimmer* and *glimpse* ; Engl. *gleam*, a ray of light ; Isl. *glimbr*, splendour. Taking away the *g*, we have the Gr. λαπτω, to shine ; Isl. *liome*, light ; Ulphila, *lauhmon*, lightning. And with the *g*, Swed. *glo*, to fee ; Gr. γλαυσσω ; Sax. *gloren*, splendere ; hence Scot. *glowr*, to look intently at any object. So in the old Ballad :

" I canna get leave
" To luke to my luve,
" My minny's aye *glowring* owr me."

Isl. *gloggr*, and Goth *glau*, sharp-sighted ; Gr. γληνν, pupil of the eye; Fr. *glaire*, the clear or white of the egg; Isl. *glæ*, the shining of the ocean in a calm. Hence Gr. γαληνr, serenitas; γαληνοω, sereno; γλμνια, res nitidæ, prætiosæ; γληνος, a star; Swed. *gran*, shining; whence the *Apollo Gryneus*, literally the *Splendid Sun*. We are much deceived if the many coincidences we have here thrown together, (and to which more might easily be added) do not prove very strongly, a primitive and universal language. We have not room to alledge the many examples the Eastern dialects furnish to us ;—these we reserve for a larger work. Mean while, the reader may look at Ihre, Lex. voce *Gloa* and *Glo*.

VER. 4. *Frae*] Engl. *from*. But we have kept the true orthography. Swed. *fram*, prorsum, adverbium motus de loco posteriori in anteriorem. The *pro* of the Latins is from this root, and has the same meaning in *prorsum, procedere, prodire, profferre ;* and the Swedes say *ga fram, gisswa fram* ; Ulphila, *iddja fram*, processit ; Luke xix. 28. *framis leitl*, a little further. So, too, in the compounds, *fram-wigis*, semper ; and Luke i..18. *fram-aldrozi*, stricken in years ; Alam. *frampringan*, producere. Tatian, cap. 73.

V. 1. *franor*, further. We find in Wilking. Saga, p. 3. *Hugprydiac spæki, oc framwifi*, a genius wife and prudent; from *fram* and *wis*, wifdom; and hence *framvis*, a diviner, conjurer; Ifl. *framygdur*, a wife man; Goth. *framfus*, a petulant fellow, ever putting himfelf forward; whence Engl. *frumpifh*. To return to the Scots word *frae*, as correfponding to the Goth. *fram*, from. Chron. Ryth. p. 444.

"Huar monde *fram* androm fly."
Qui ab altero feceffit, aufugit.

Framgangu, going from, departure; Swed. *fran*. From *fram* the ingenious and learned Ihre derives *framea*, a dart ufed by the ancient Germans, mentioned by Tacitus, M. G. cap. 6. Haftas, vel ipforum vocabulo, *frameas* gerunt; from *fram* and *frumen*, mittere, jaculari. Hence, in Ulphila, we find, Joh. x. 5. *Framthjana ni lajsjand*, a ftranger will they not follow. Alam. *framider*; Ger. *fremd*, a ftranger; and Scot. *fremdman*, one come from far.

Douglas writes this word fometimes *fra* and *fray*.

Whang] Prim. *tan*, a binding or cord. Hence every thing of a long narrow fhape. *Whang*, a flice of cheefe, cut in a long narrow form. Ulphila, *twang*; Ifl. *tange*, vinculum; Swed. *tang*, a ftrap hanging at the handle of a knife. They alfo call an ifthmus *tang*, and we fay a *tongue of land*. Ifl. *thuing*, a band; A. S. *twang*, whence our *whang*.

The primitive *tan* is found in all the Scythian dialects, and thofe derived from them. Swed. *tan*, nerve. Leg, Goth. cap. 22. *Thau en fundr er than hels edanacca*; Si abfciffus fuerit nervus colli. Welch *tant*, chorda; Ger. id. Alam. *than*, a leather ftrap; A. S. *tan*, vimen, virgultum; and hence *tanhlyta*, fortilegus. Swed. *tanor*, filaments in flefh. The Gr. τενω, is formed from *tan*, fign. a nerve.—Odyff. 3.

" — τελεκυς

The prieving was good, it pleas'd them baith,
To lo'e her for ay, he gae her his aith,
                                                    Quo'

" — πελεκυς διεκοψε τενον]ας,
" Αυχενας.——

Securis abscidit nervos cervicis. The Islanders call the nets for catching birds *thaner*; and hence Latin *tenus, tenq-ris*, in Nonius; and Plaut. Bacchid. v. v. 6.

" Pendebit hodie pulcre; ita intendi *tenus.*"

It is needless to observe that our *tendon* is derived from the same source. The Goths call the swaddling bands of children *tanom*; Chron. Rythm. p. 561. *Barn then som an i ta-nom lag*, Children that lay yet in their swaddling bands. The Greeks called them τενια, τενιδια. Vide Jun. Gloss. Ulph. p. 330.

VER. 5. *Prieving*] The proof, the first taste of any thing. Primitive is *por, pro*; Celt. *por*, what is *before*; as *por* signifies also *face*. Hence *porro, probo, probation*; Fr. *preuve, eprouver*, the *prow* of a ship; Gr. πρω]ος; Lat. *primus, prior, princeps*, and a vast number of other words. At present we confine ourselves to the northern dialects, where we find, in the Celtic, *prid*; whence our *price*, or value of any thing; Ger. *preis*; Lat. *pretium*; Italian *apprezzare*; Goth. *pris*, id. and metaphorically, glory, honour, high esteem; whence Engl. *praise*. The truly learned and elegant Ihre observes, that, in the old Swio-Gothic, they used *prishet* in the same sense. In Chron. Ryth. p. 442.

" *Och innan strid stor prishet was.*"
In war he was greatly prized.

Quo' she, to leave thee I will be laith,
   My winsom Gaberlunzie-man.

IX.

With them *prisa*, sign. *to prize, apprize*; and these words clearly indicate their northern origin. Hence, too, Fr. *priser, mepriser*; *winna priset*, to win the prize. In our dialect *pris, prieve*, is proof, or trial, as here; and in Douglass, p. 309. 49.

"Thus rude examplis may we gif,
"Thocht God be his awin Creauture to *prieve*."

We also use the verb, to *prie*, to taste.

VER. 5. *Baith*] Engl. both, by a faulty pronunciation; for the primitive is found in Ulphila's, *ba, bai*, i. e. *baith*, not *both*. So Luke 5. v. 7. *Ba tho skipa gasullidedun*, they filled both the ships; and Luke 6. v. 39. *Bai in dalga driusand*, both will fall into the ditch. A. S. *ba, butu*; Alam. *bedu, beidu*; Isl. *bathur*. It is diverting to see Junius gravely supposing that our word comes from Gr. $\alpha\mu\varphi\omega$, as if our ancestors could not reckon *two*, till the Greeks taught them. The savages of Kamschatka do more than this; for they follow the number of their fingers and toes up to twenty, and having got thus far, they stop, and cry, Where shall I find more? See the account of this country, published at Petersburg, and translated by Grieve, p. 178. We just add, that the same observation may be applied to the words, *aith*, oath, *laith*, loth, which occur in the verses immediately following, and which have been equally vitiated by our southern neighbours, as this word *baith*.

VER. 7. *Laith*] Loth. But ours is the true pronunciation, as derived from Al. *leid, luad*; Alam. *lath*; Belg. *leyd,*

leyd, odious, ugly, troublefome; Old Danifh, *tha the læwas and lædedon iuch*, who hate and perfecute you. The primitive of all thefe is found in the Celt. *lad, loc,* to cut, pain, or wound; Bafg. *laceria,* misfortune. We cannot deny ourfelves the pleafure of following this original through fome of its many defcendants; hence come Gr. λῃδειν; Fr. *lacerer*; Lat. *lacerare,* our *lacerate*; Fr. *loqueté,* cut out in flices; whence our *lock* of hair, or wool; Celt. *laza,* to kill; and hence *lay,* a poem on any tragical fubject; fo Dougl. 321. v. 5.

"The dowy tones, and layes lamentabil."

Ital. *lai,* and our *lament,* the true Scots appellation of Elegiac fongs; A. S. *ley,* id. which neither Menage, nor even Skinner underftood; Ger. *lied,* a fong, but properly a melancholy ditty; as the B. L. *leudus* alfo fignifies; Fortunat. Epift. ad Gregor. Turon. ad Lib. 1. Poemat. Sola fœpe bombicans barbaros *leudos* harpa relidebat. Id. Lib. 7. Poem 8.

"Nos tibi verficulos, dent barbara carmina *leudos*."

Hence, too, Lat. *leſſus,* and the Baf. Bret. *lais,* a melancholy found or cry; *e-legia, e-legy, lefion*; and the Fr. *leze majeſteè,* high treafon. We could eafily bring many more proofs of the truth of our account of the term *elegy,* as that paſſage of Proclus, in Chreft. ap. Phot. Bibl. Το γαρ θρηνος, ελεγιαν ελεγων οι παλαιοι, veteres luctum vocarunt ελεγον. Ovid gives us the fame idea, Ded. de Lib. 3. Eleg. 1.

"Flebilis indignos elegia folve capillos,
"Heu nimis ex vero nunc tibi nomen ineft."

Voſſius (in Elegia) has quoted thefe paſſages, but gives no Etymology, as indeed the root is loſt both in the Greek and Roman languages. But we muſt ftop, after obferving that the

Fr.

IX.

O kend my minny I war wi' you,
Ill-fardly wad she crook her mou',

Sic

Fr. words *læid*, (which of old signified, offence, injury, and now *ugliness*,) *laideur, laidron*, and the Gr. λοιδορεω, to defame, are all of this family.

VER. 8. *Winsom*] We have have already shewn the meaning and origin of this word, in the note on Stanza II. ver. 6. In the old ballads we find it often used; so in the old song of Gilderoy, (Percy, vol. I. p. 324, 325.) My *winsom* Gilderoy; Ger. *minnesam*, from *minne*, love, which we have already explained; Alam. *wino*, a friend; A. S. *vine*, beloved.

STANZA IX.

VER. 1. *Kend*] The primitive *kan-enen*, signifies art, knowledge, dexterity. Hebr. *gwanen*, an inchanter, and the verb *gwenen*, to divine; Gr. κυνειν; Gaelic *kann*, I know; *kunna, kenning*, knowledge; *kennimen*, knowing, learned men, priests; Ulphila, *kunnan*, Mark 4. v. 11. *Iswis attiban ist, kunnan runa thiud angardjos Goths,*—To you it is given to know the mystery of the Kingdom of God. Isl. *kunna;* Alam. *kennen, chennen*; from *kunna*, the English *cunning;* in sea-phrase, to *cunn a ship*, is to direct her course; in Fr. *maitre gonin*, a sharper. See the poor efforts of Menage to explain this word. Hesych. κυννειν, ςυνιεναι, επιςαϑαι, to understand. We say here *kenspeckled*, easy to be known by particular marks. The Goths use a similar phrase, *Kenespak, qui alios facile agnoscit*; Ihre in *kenn*.

VER. 2. *Ill-fardly*] Ill-favouredly, in an ugly manner. In Engl. well-favoured, handsome, well-looking; and thus

our

our tranflators of the Bible ufe it, Gen. xli. v. 3. 4. Primitive is *fa*, to eat, to feed on good things, as defcended from the family of *fa*, denoting every action belonging to the mouth, as eating, fpeaking, &c. So the Latin *fari*, whence Fr. *faribole*, idle tale, and the like. From *fa* comes Latin *favus*, honey-comb; *favere alicui*, to favour one; our *favourite*, *favour*; Fr. *favorifer*, *fauteur*, and the Latin *fautor*. The common word *infant*, Latin *infans*, comes not from *in* and *fari*, one who cannot fpeak, as our herd of Lexicographers fay, but from *fa*, to nourifh, to feed, whence *fari* itfelf is derived, which being a diffyllable, can never be a primitive, thofe (as we have elfewhere obferved) being all *monofyllables*, in every language. From this root, too, we have *fawn*, a young deer. N. B. The animals do not fpeak, therefore it is impoffible that *fawn* can come from Latin *fari*: but we muft ftop here, left we offend thofe who hold, that the Ourang-outans, a fpecies of the monkey, belong to the human race; and that, though they have paffed above fix thoufand years without framing a language, it is ftill *very rationally expected*, that they will yet form one, (vide Origin and Prog. of Lang. vol. I. p. 189. 272). Whenever we are happy enough to poffefs a Dictionary, collected by fome learned Ouranoutang, and a Grammar of this new fpeech, we nothing doubt, but we fhall difcover many primitives of language yet unknown. But this by the bye.

We find *favour*, in the Welch, *fleafor*, *flawr*, and in the Greek, φαω, φημι; and in what Feftus writes, *faventia*, bonam ominationem fignificat; *favere*, enim, eft *bona fari*. Hence the folemn form, *Favete linguis*. Voffius has faid much, to no purpofe, about this, in *Favere*; but he had no principles. We fee new proofs of the truth of our Etymology in the *hinnuleus* of the Latins, and the Gr. νεος, fig. παιδος, a *boy* or *young one*. Vide Salmaf. Plin. Exercit. p. 106. and

Spelman, in *Fenatio* and *Foinefium*. Lye mentions *fauntekin* as an old English word, fignifying an infant or little boy, which he rightly derives from the Iflandic *fante*, a young man; whence the Italian *fante*, a page or fervant, and the French *fantaffin*, a foldier who ferves on foot, and of thofe whom we call *in-fantry*.

VER. 2. *Crook*] Prim. Celt. *Crok*, fignifies every thing that takes hold; and as nothing can take hold but what deviates from the ftreight line, this word has formed a very numerous family: Goth. *krok*; the Gael. *krock*, *kruick*, an earthen pot or vafe; Goth. *kruka*, id. We in Scotland call the iron on which the kettle hangs a *crook*. Shepherd's *crook*, from its bent form; and, for the fame reafon, *crotchet* in mufic fignifies a note, with a tail turned up. Hence, too, come the French *crotcheteur efcroi*, a thief who feizes every thing he can lay hands on; *croffe*, the fheep-hook, with which bifhops are invefted; *acrocher*, to feize or lay hold of. Gebelin obferves, with his ufual acutenefs, that the French peafants who revolted in 1598, were called *Les Croquans*, becaufe they plundered and carried off every thing wherever they came.

Mou'] Mouth. Prim. *muth*, *mun*; whence Ulphila has *munths*, the mouth; Celt. *mu*, id. alfo the lips. Hence Fr. *mot*, what is fpoken with the lips; *motet*, Bafq. *motafa*, found of the voice; Gr. μυδ҅ος, and *mythology*; *murmur*, i. e. mu-mu, fmall found made by the mouth. Our old word *mump* comes from the fame origin; alfo *mant*, to ftammer From the ancient Celtic and Welch *mant*, fignifying the jaw-bone, comes the Latin *mandibula*, and the ancient *munio*, *munito*, to eat; Feft. *munitio*, *mortificatio*, ciborum; alfo *mando*, *manduco*; the Fr. *manger*; Ital. *mangiere*; Gr. μυδ҅ζ .'', loqui. Ihre informs us, that the mouths of rivers are called *Mynne-a-mynne*, and Ifl. *munne*, from *mun*, the mouth. They fay alfo, the *mouth* and *lips* of

a

Sic a pure man she'd nevir trow,
After the Gaberlunzie-man.

My

a wound, as we do: Ll. Scaniæ, p. 22. *Far man far gonum lar, allar lag, allar arm, swa at that havir twa munna*, If any man's thigh, leg, or arm, be so wounded as that the sore shall have two mouths. In the same sense the French use *balafre*, a great wound, which Dutchat rightly derives from the old French *balevre*, bilabrum: Ce qu'on appelle *balafre*, est proprement une grande playe, qui fait une espece de *bouche*, et par consequent *deux levres*. The Gothic *munhasteis*, a set form of words, and used in their ancient Jurisprudence. Vide Ihre, Lex. in voce, vol. II. p. 207.

We have in this word a clear example of the method the first men took to express opposite ideas, without multiplying the primitive words. *Muth* first denoted the mouth and speech. They formed the negative by using the same word in the opposite signification, and thus *muth* came to signify a *dumb person*; Gr. μυδος; Lat. *mutus*, whence our *mute*; The Hebrew *muth*, a dead man, one who speaks not. In another work we have collected many examples of this kind, which we have no room for here. Such is the word *alt*, high; whence the Lat. *altus*, signifying *high*, and also *deep*.

VER. 3. *Trow*] The verb, *to believe*; Belg. *truen*, id. Douglas uses *trueles*, for faithless. Prim. Goth. *trost*, trust, fidelity. Hence, metaphorically, *a bold man*, on whom we may well rely. So Chron. Ryth. p. 311.

" *Thet var en godn trost man.*"
He was a good and trusty man.

Isl. *traustor*, Alam. *gidrost*, Engl. *trusty*. Otfrid, l. 5. cap. 23.

My dear, quod he, zére ʒet o'wr zoung,
An' hae na learn'd the beggar's tongue,

To

"Zi themo thronoste,
"Sie sint al *gidroste.*"

In their service all were faithful. Germ. *triest*, and Swed. *dristig*; vide Ihre in *Dristig*. From this root, too, the Greeks formed ϑαρσος and ϑαρσεω, *to dare*, or more properly, *to be confident*, by a literary metathesis of the same kind as that used by the Goths, while they say *toras*, to dare; *jators*, I dare, and then *trost*, our *trust*. So the ancient Greeks said indifferently, ϑασος, ϑρασυς, ϑαρσυια, and ϑρασυνω, audacem reddo. Ulph. *thrasslian*, to confide or trust, and *dauran*, dare; Mark xii. 34. *gawdarsta*, audebat, which the Allemans pronounced *gidorsta*. In one of the Church Hymns, n. 127, *The lofwade Gud med gladje och trost*, They praised God with gladness and confidence. We observe, by the way, that our Scots phrase of *loving* God, used for *praising* him, frequent in Robert Bruce's Life, and other ancient poems, is formed from the Goth. *lofware*, to praise. In the Barb. Latin Laws, we find often the phrases, *Trustis regius*, *Esse in truste regia*, *Trustinus*; and the like; all denoting loyalty. Vid. Cange in *Trustis*. Marculf. For. l. 1. 18. These men were also called *Antrustiones*. Vid. Leg. Sal. Tit. 32. cap. 20. edit. Heroldi. Marculf. Lib. 1. Form. 47. ibi Lindenbrog. Gloss. The *Antrustiones* were of high dignity in the King's Court, as we gather from the article of the Gaelic Law last cited. We have the verb *traist*, to trust, frequent in Douglas. So p. 52. v. 25.

―― "And there traist coistis nyce."

And p. 213. 37.

"His traisty faith."――

VER.

To fallow me frae toun to toun,
And carry the Gaberlunzie on.

X.

Wi' kauk and keel I'll win zour bread,
And spinnels and quhorles for them wha need,
Whilk

VER. 7. *Frae toun to toun*] By *toun* here is not solely meant *city*, in which sense we now use it; but the Scots apply this word to every little village, and even to a farm-house, where there is an inclosed yard, after the manner of their ancestors, from the prim. *dun*, A. S. *tun*, Alam. *zun*, all signifying an inclosure. Hence the Belgic *tuyn*, a garden, literally an inclosure; Gael. *dun-dunam*, to inclose; A. S. *tynan*, *betynan*, id. The first cities of our Celtic and Saxon ancestors were only farm-houses, or a few straggling hutts, inclosed with rails. Tacitus de M. G. cap. 16. Nullis Germanorum populis urbes habitari notum est, nec pati quidem inter se junctas sedes, (forte ædes) vicos locant, non in nostrum morem connexis et coherentibus ædificiis. These *vici* were separate houses, like our farmers *steddings*, which we still call *towns*. In some districts they are called *mains*, from *mansio*, and the B. Latin *mansus*, a *manse*, now restricted to our parsons houses.

STANZA X.

VER. 1. *Kauk*] From the primitive *cal*, *cel*, every thing hard and proper to inclose with. Hence Latin *celare*,
cellarium,

cellarium, our *cellar;* French *celer,* our *con-ceal;* the Celtic *cal,* a hut or ſtable. Hence *kal* came to denote the materials for incloſing, *viz.* ſtones, and eſpecially that ſoft kind of ſtone, eaſily divided into ſmall pieces, which the Engliſh call *chalk,* and we, more properly, pronounce *kauk.* Iſl. *kalk;* Gael. *calch;* Alam. *calc;* A. S. *ceale, ceale, ſtan.* From this root, too, comes the Greek χαλιξ, explained by Suidas, μικρον λιθιδιον, a little ſtone, and more clearly by Heſych. χαλικες, οἱ εις τα οικοδομας μικροι λιθοι ; of the ſame kind was the χαλιξ, mentioned by Thucidides, in his Account of the Walls of the Pyreus, built by the Athenians, in lib. 1. We are indebted to the induſtry of Junius for this remark; yet he does not even attempt an etymology of the word χαλιξ, which has baffled all the lexicographers.

Keel] A red calcarious ſtone, uſed by carpenters for marking their lines on wood. The promiſe here made by the feigned Gaberlunzie-man, to get a livelihood for his ſweet-heart by *kauk* and *keel,* alludes to the practice of fortune-tellers in Scotland, who uſually pretend to be dumb, to gain credit with the vulgar, and therefore have recourſe to ſigns made with kauk and keel, to explain their meaning. The primitive is plainly the ſame with that of *kauk;* *col, cel,* a ſmall ſtone, (of a red colour).

Win] In the more modern acceptation, ſimply ſignifies to gain. So the Goths uſe *vinna* of one who *wins* at play, or in making bargains, or by gaining his cauſe in a court of juſtice; *winna et kæromal,* in cauſa ſuperiorem eſſe. Vide Ihre, vol. II. col. 2020. But of old it ſignified to *gain our bread by hard labour,* and induſtry. This is ſtill its common meaning in the Iſlandic. So Exod. 15. *Winna alladina winna,* Thou ſhalt work all thy work. Hence *winnubiu,* a labouring man. Numbers, cap. 30. A. S. *vinnan.* So the Dutch ſay *land winnen,* to plough the ground. *Winnende leeden,* membra genitalia ;

Iſl.

Isl. *vinna*, labour; in the A. S. *vinfull*, industrious; *win-lagga*, sign. to give one's self a great deal of trouble. Hence it is used to denote suffering. So Ulphila, Mark viii. 31. *Skal sunus mans silu vinnam*, The son of man must suffer many things: And Luke ii. 48. *Sa atta theins, ja ik vinnandona sokidedum thuk*, Thy father and I have sought thee sorrowing. Hence it is transferred to child-bearing: Swed. *Hon har wunnet en son*, She has born a son; and Belg. *Kinderin gewinnen*, to bring forth children.

As the ancients knew of no other honourable gains, besides the spoils acquired in war, hence *winna* came to denote conquest, victory in war; and hence our phrase *to win the battle*, to win the field. In Matth. xxiv. 7. Vers. Ulph. *Theod vinth ongean theode*, Nation shall fight against nation. *Gevinn*, war; *gevinne*, battle. Tatian, cap. 195. 4. *Mine ambathti wunnin*, My servants would fight. In an old Runic inscription, quoted by Ihre (in *Winna*), *Vant Selalant ala*, He conquered all Seland. The most modern signification is that in which it is applied to *gain* in general. From *winna*, applied to war, comes the Latin *vincere*. Strange! that Vossius did not see the true etymon, though he has mentioned the Goth. *winnen*, in *Vinco*. But he seldom or never looks further than the Greek or Latin. Still more absurd is Varro's etymon, lib. 4. de L. L. *Victoria*, ab eo quod superati vincuntur. Yet this Varro pretended to give us the origin of language; and he is generally called *Romanorum Doctissimus*; and so, perhaps, he was.

VER. 2. *Spinnels*] Goth. *spindel*, Machina tornatorum, in gyrum versatilis, says the learned Professor of Upsal. *Slenda*, fusus, *spincok*, fusus, colus; and hence our *rok*, a distaff. A. S. *spinel*; and from spindle the Greek ςπονδυλος, as the spindle is of a long slender form; the Goth. *spinkog*, sig. *slender*; and, by a similar figure, we say *spindle-shanks*,

of

of a man underlimbed. The prim. is *span*, to extend, or draw out to length, as the thread is extended from the mass on the diſtaff. Hence our *span*, of the hand *extended*. Vid. Bullet, Dict. Celt. in *Span*. We have much to ſay concerning this primitive, which we reſerve for our Scoto-Gothic Gloſſary. Suffice it to obſerve here, that the word *span*, to extend, and hence to meaſure, is found in all the dialects of the North. A. S. *span*, *ſpon*, *ſponne*; Alam. *ſpana*; Iſl. *ſpan*, *ſpon*; Ital. *ſpanna*; Fr. *eſpan*, *empan*. Vide Hicks, Gram. Franc. p. 98. The Swed. verb *ſpanna*, to meaſure. Hence they call grain in general *ſpannemal*, as being ſold by meaſure. Of a young ſlender girl they ſay, *Hon ar ſa ſmal, att man kan ſpanna om benne*, She is ſo ſmall, that with two ſpans you may encircle her; *ſpanna konut*, mulieres contrectare. We are not ſure whether we are to connect with this the Goth. *ſpann*, a bracelet; Ger. *ſpange*, B. Lat. *ſpanga*, de qua Cange. From this word comes Swed. *ſpanna*, to bind. Feſtus has *ſpinter*, armillæ genus. *Spannabalt* was the ancient deſperate mode of duelling, when the combatants, bound within the narrow circle of one belt, which ſurrounded both, attacked each other with ſhort daggers. From *ſpin*, *ſpan*, a number of words have their origin, all denoting what is long, ſlender, and ſharp. Such are Goth. *ſpik*, whence our *ſpike* and *handſpike*, the wooden leavers by which ſeamen heave at the capſtan. The Lat. *ſpica*, *ſpiculum*; Gael. *ſpeice*; *ſpoke* of a wheel; Ital. *ſpighe*, della rota; Ger. *ſpeiche*. In the Armor. *ſpec* and *anſpec*, ſign. a ſmall leaver. The Gothic *ſpik*, a ſpear; whence the *ſpiculum* of the Latins. Confer Cange, in *Specillum*, a probe.

Quhorles] A perforated piece of circular ſtone, fixed on the ſpindle to give it weight in turning round; literally, *whirlers*, to encreaſe the motion in *whirling* round. Scyth. *whirra*, *horra*, *wherta*, turbare, tumultuari, ſurſum et deorſum ferri. Goth.

Whilk is a gentle trade indeed,
To carry the Gaberlunzie on.
I'll bow my leg and crook my knee,
An' draw a black clout owr my eye,

A

Goth. *huirfwel,* our *whirlwind,* from *hwerfwa,* Isl. *huerfa,* in gyrum agere. From the Goth. *horra,* the English *hurry.* Prim. *girwhir,* circle. A. S. *ymbbærtan,* to be turned round. Belg. *werwen, wieren.* Hence the sea-phrase, *to wear ship,* to bring her round. Fr. *virer* and *verve,* by which 'they denote the *furor poeticus,* which strongly agitates the mind ; and this affection the Islanders, among whom of old it was very strong and frequent, call *scaldwingl.* From this primitive the Greek γυρυν, and the Latin *gyrare.* It is remarkable that the old Latins said *vervare,* for *circumagere ;* and *urvare,* to draw the circular line with the plough, to mark the boundaries of the future city. The word is pure Gothic ; but neither Festus, nor any of his commentators, understood it. Confer Acta Sueciæ Litterar. vol. IV. p. 386. Junius has given us no etymon of *whirl.* Vid. in voce.

VER. 6. *Clout*] Goth. *klut,* panni frustum, a rag. The prim. is *clo-clu,* covered, shut up. Hence Lat. *claudo, cludo, in-cludo,* and our *close, inclose, disclose.* Douglas used *cloys* for *cloister,* place where monks and nuns are shut up. In the Gael. *cluff,* in A. S. *cleof,* signify joining of a rent. A. S. *geclutad hraegl,* a clouted garment. " Ex his conjicere licet (says Ihre) *klut,* prima et antiquissim significatione denotasse panni frusta ad sarciendas vestes immissa." In English, a *clouterly fellow,* a mean man, a fellow in rags. Belg. *kloets,* a fool ; Swed. *klutare,* a botcher of old clothes.

K   VER.

A cripple or blind they will ca' me,
While we will be merry and fing.

VER. 7. *Cripple*] Lame man. A word found in all the Celtic dialects. -Welfh *crupl*; A. S. *crypl*; Belg. *krepel*, *kreupel*; Swed. *krympling*, paralytic, membris captus; whence our *cramp*, binding of the finews. The primitive is *craf*, *crif*, *craw*, to bind. Hence Gaelic *crampa*, French *crampon*, *cramponer*. The fhell-fifh *crab*, from its claws, and the French *crapaud*, are of the fame origin. Hence, too, Greek γρυπαινειν, in-curvari, γρυπαλιον, a man bent down or crippled with age. Gloff. Philoxeni κραιπαλοντες, vacillantes. Junius odly deduces *cripple*, a κραιπαλν, crápula:—But we are weary of his blunders; and fo, perhaps, is the reader of ours.

——*Jam fatis eft, manum de tabula.*

ADDENDA.

ADDENDA.

FOR the following elucidations of the general principles laid down in the Preface, and exemplified in the Notes on the foregoing Ballad, the Public and I are indebted to a learned and worthy friend of the Author*, whose extensive erudition is only equalled by the modesty and candour conspicuous in his whole deportment. I am sure our learned readers will regret with me, that he has not pushed his researches further than he has done. But, from the little he has here given us, the general principle of Etymology I have endeavoured to establish will derive new force, and our readers new entertainment.

TO THE READER.

IN the following strictures, I have, in a manner, confined myself to the Oriental languages. My knowledge of the Northern tongues is too much bounded to qualify me for pursuing the coincidences of words through their various dialects. I shall, perhaps, be blamed for terminating the origin of too great a number of words in the Hebrew. This, however, I did, from a conviction that their radical syllables and significations appeared most obvious in that language. In a few instances I have taken the liberty to differ from the learned

---

* Mr *David Doig*, Rector of the Academy in Stirling.

learned and laborious Author of the Notes. I have not, however, the remoteſt intention to detract from his well-known abilities and merit. I imagined it might neither be diſpleaſing to himſelf, nor his readers, to ſee, upon ſome occaſions, the ſame individual term placed in various points of light. If the unlearned philologer ſhall acquire one new idea by the peruſal of them, I ſhall think myſelf abundantly rewarded for the pains I have taken in throwing them together.

Before I proceed to the additional notes, I ſhall take the liberty to preſent to the reader one ſingle word, which, in my opinion, furniſhes a very ſtriking evidence of the truth of the Author's leading principle, with relation to the exiſtence of an original univerſal language.

Ur, aur, our] Theſe words ſignify *fire, light, heat,* and ſeveral other things nearly connected with theſe ideas. They occur frequently in the Hebrew, and its ſiſter-dialects. In the Chald. we have *Ur*, the name of a city, where, it is thought, the Sun was worſhipped by a perpetual *fire.* Alſo *Or-choe,* the ſeat of the Chaldean aſtronomers called *Orcheni,* Strabo, l. 16. p. 739. We find *oreitæ,* or *oritæ,* in different parts of the Eaſt, the Chald. *Atun B-ura,* the furnace of *fire,* occurs, Dan. chap. 3. ver. 6. &c. In the Gentoo language *war,* which is only a ſmall variation, imports *day, light, ſee*—Halhed's Pref. to his Tranſlation of the Gentoo Laws. In the ſame tongue, the moſt ancient Dynaſty of the Gentoo Princes were called *Surage,* from *Sur,* a name or epithet of the *Sun*—See Halhed's Pref. and Col. Dow's Introd. to the Hiſt. of Hindoſtan.

In the old Perſian, or Pehlvi, the word *hyr* ſignifies *fire,* the ſame with *ur,* only with the aſpirate prefixed.

Hyr-bad, a fire, temple ; *Az-ur,* Mars, i. e. the *fiery* planet, compounded of *Az,* or *Aſh,* fire, and *Ur,* heat or light. *Hur,* or *Chur,* is a common name of the Sun in that

language.

language. *Kur*, *Rafch*, *Horefh*, Κυρος, Gr. which laſt, Plut. Vit. Artax. ſignifies the Sun. From the ſame word we have the firſt ſyllable of *Or-mazd*, the God of Light, the chief Divinity of the Perſians. Here, too, we find *Purim*, ſignifying *lots*, denominated from the ceremonies of *fire* employed upon theſe occaſions—Eſth. chap. iii. ver. 7. &c.

The Arabian *Uro-talt*, Herod. l. 3. cap. 8. is compounded of *ur*, light, and *jalath*, high. In Egypt we find *Orus*, or *Horus*, Apollo, the Sun, Herod, l. 2. Diod. Sic. l. 1. Plut. Iſis and Oſiris, Horapollo, Paſſ. In the ſame language we have *Athur*, the name of a month, partly anſwering to our October, on the 17th day of which Oſiris was put into the coffin, a word compounded of *ait*, or *at*, or *ath*, heat, and *ur*, or *or*—See Plut. ubi ſupra. The particle *pi* was common in the Egyptian tongue, ſee Kirch. Prolegom. Copt. page 180, 297. Jameſon's Spicileg. cap. 9. parag. 4. Hence *pur*, fire, and ſometimes the Sun. Of this word, and the Hebrew *chamud*, or *omud*, columna, is compounded the term πυραμις, pyramid, edifices, erected in honour of the Sun.

The πυρ of the Greeks, according to Plato (Cratyl. p. 410. Serr.) was borrowed from the Phrygians. Theſe laſt had received it from the Perſians by the Armenians, who ſpoke nearly the ſame language. The word πυρ produced a numerous family, all deſcendants of the oriental term *Ur*.

Or.] Another modification of the ſame word, produced ὡρα, tempeſtas, a ſeaſon, with a numerous train of connections. Alſo ὡρα, beauty; αορ, a ſword, from its glittering, by the ſame analogy that the Scandinavians call it *brandt*: Alſo ὁραω, video, and many others.

From *aur* we have the Eolic αυρα, αυρος, afterwards adopted by the Latins. From *our* we have ουρος, ventus ſecundus, with all its compounds and derivatives; alſo κυροςυρα, the North Pole-Star, which the Greeks have corrupted in a ſhameful

shameful manner. It is really compofed of the Hebrew or Phœnician *kanes*, congregavit, and *ur*, light, i. e. an *Affemblage of Light*. From the fame root we have ουρανος, cœlum. The laft part is probably the oriental *en*, fignifying an *eye*, a fountain, the Sun being the eye of Heaven, or fountain of light.

In the Latin tongue we have a numerous tribe of words defcended from *ur, or, aur;* fuch are *uro, buro, burrum,* ap. Feftum pro *rufum, purus, purgo*. From the fame root we have *furo*, to rage like fire ; *furia*, a fury. Perhaps this laft word may be a native of Egypt, from whence the Greeks derived their ideas of the infernal regions. See Diod. Sic. l. 1. juxta finem. The Latian Jupiter was called Jupiter *Puer*. I fufpect this epithet is diftorted from *pi-ur*. In ancient times, it is probable, this Deity was no other than the *Sun*. See Macrob. Saturn. cap. 17. His Minifters were called *Pueri;* and becaufe they were generally handfome young men, felected for that office, in procefs of time, I fancy, the word *puer* came to fignify a young man in general. At Prenefte, *Jupiter Puer* was in high veneration ; he prefided over the celebrated Sortes Preneftini, defcribed by Cicero, de Divinat. l. 2. From *or* we have *orior, ordior*, and perhaps *oro ;* from *aur* we have *aura, Aurora, aurum,* &c.

The words *fire, air*, &c. plainly defcended of the fame ftock, under various forms, and with new modifications, pervade all the German and Scandinavian dialects ; an affertion which the Author of the Notes would certainly have demonftrated, had that term occurred in the text of the Ballad.

In the French we have *jour*, with all its compounds, from the very fame root. In the Celtic, *ore*, or *aur*, fignifies *gold*, concerning which, Voffius (Etym. V. *Aurum*) has told a heap of abfurdites. The name *ore* is given it in allufion to its fhining quality, a word which we have adopted,

and

and applied to signify any metal before it is purified and refined. *Aur* also in Celtic signifies *yellow*. Vid, Bullet in *Aur*. Those who are well acquainted with the remains of the ancient Celtic, can, no doubt, produce many other cognates of the same original term. If the above detail should be thought tedious, the best apology I can make is, that I am confident I have, for the sake of brevity, omitted at least one third of what I could easily have produced: At the same time, all these analogies might have been confirmed and elucidated by a variety of quotations from ancient and modern authors, had the bounds I have prescribed to myself admitted such enlargements.

TITLE.

Gaber] In some places of Scotland, this word, among the vulgar, denotes an idea very different from that assigned by the Author of the Notes. When a thing is dashed to pieces, they say it is driven to *gaberts*, or *gabers*. According to this acceptation, the *Gaberlunzie-man* will imply a fellow whose clothes about his loins are all rags and tatters, all worn out, &c.

The character exhibited throughout the Ballad, seems rather to be that of a common *beggar* than of a *tinker*, though indeed both professions were often united in the same person.

Gab seems originally to denote the roof of the mouth or palate. In some of the Eastern languages it signifies an *eminence*, a *protuberance*, *gibbous*, &c. Hence Arab. *gebal*, a hill; also the Lat. *gibbus*, hump-backed. According to this idea, it was appropriated to signify the roof *of the mouth*, which, indeed, rises in a *gibbous* form or arch over the tongue and lower part of the mouth. From the notion of a rising protuberance, it was probably transferred to signify *cabbage*, and whatever else imports *eminence*, *elevation*, or *gibbosity*.

Hence

Hence *gabah*, *scyphus*, a kind of cup, so called from its *gibbous protuberant* belly, perhaps the origin of the Scotch word *cap*, and of all its German and Scandinavian cognates.

Caph, Hebr. the *hollow of the hand*, or any other *cavity* fitted for containing. By changing the *ph* but a very little, we have *cav*, *gau*, *cow*, and *gow*, syllables which occur in a number of compounds, both in the East and West. Plut. in Alex. tells us that *gau-gamela* signifies the house of the camel. It were easy to trace this word through many different languages. It is the origin of the English word *cave*, Scotch *cove*, and Welch *cowe*; Lat. *cavus*, *a-um*, hollow. Here, I believe, we may discover a composition of the word *cælum* very different from that usually assigned. *Co* is a house, and *El*, or *Il*, a Phœnician name of the Deity. Hence we have Ennius's *Allisonans Cœil*, Annal. L. 1. and also the following verses:

" *Coilum* prospexit stellis fulgentibus aptum.
" Olim de *Coilo* laivum dedit inclytus signum,
" Saturnus quem *Coilus* genuvit.
" Unus erat quem tu tollas in coirila *Coili*
" Templa."

Hence it is probable that *Co-il* originally signified the House of *Il*, or *El*, which is perfectly conformable to the notion of Heaven commonly exhibited in Scripture. The idea annexed to this word carries us back to a very uncultivated state of Society. The same word being applied both to signify a *cave* and a *house*, intimates that the original men often dwelt in *caves*. Vid. the Poems of Ossian, passim.

" Domus antra fuerunt,
" Et densi frutices, vinetæ cortice virgæ."
Ovid. Metam.

ADDENDA.

As *gow, gaw, caw, cow,* originally fignified a *houfe,* in procefs of time it came to import a collection of *houfes,* a *village,* a *city*. This was the cafe both in the German and Celtic tongues. Thus we have *Cra-cow, Tor-gaw, Wormes-gaw, Nord-gaw, Rhin-gaw*: See Cluv. Germ. Antiq. l. 1. cap. 13. p. 91. Confer Bullet in *Gouri,* and *Gowrin.* In Scotland we have *Glaf-cow,* or *Glaf-gow, Linlith-gow,* &c. In the old Britifh dialect, *gowe,* or rather *cowe,* fignified likewife *low, hollow;* Scotch *howe.* From *gow,* or *cow,* and *ri,* a *river,* we have *Gowrie,* a low fertile tract of ground, lying on the north bank of the river Tay. In ancient times, this diftrict lay between the rivers Tay and Erne.

Lunzie] We call a bulky parcel, which one carries on his *haunch,* under his coat, a *lunchick;* perhaps the fame with the Englifh *luncheon,* both derived from the word *lunzie.*

STANZA I.

VER. 1. *The*] This particle has a moft extenfive range both in the Eaftern and Weftern parts of the Globe. Hebr. *zah,* or *zahah;* Chald. *da, di, dik, din.* Arab. Syr. much the fame. Perf. *di.* From the Chald. *da,* the Greeks formed their τ, the article of the neuter gender. It is the fame with the Latin *de,* though of a different fignification. The fame article runs through all the Gothic dialects, with very little variation.

Over] This prepofition, however meanly it figures in our dialects, is, notwithftanding, one of the terms which made a part of the original language of mankind. In Hebrew we have *chabar,* or, as fome pronounce it, *obar,* tranfivit, tranfgreffus eft; *heber,* tranfitus; Chald. *cheber, chiber,* from which word, fome think the pofterity of Abraham were called

Hebrews,

Hebrews, transfluviani, men from beyond the river. Syrian *chabara,* or *abara,* whence *Beth-abara, the houſe of the paſſage, the ferry-houſe,* John, chap. i. 25. Hence alſo *chebar,* in Ezek. From *Chabar,* trans, *over,* were denominated the *Chabareni,* a people beyond the mountains of Armenia, Steph. Byzan. in Voc.

From the Chald. *Chiber,* we have all the *Iberi* in the Eaſt. In Spain we have *Celt-iberi,* i. e. the Celtæ beyond the mountains; the river *Iber,* now *Ebro,* denominated, I ſuppoſe, by the Gauls who ſettled in that country.

The word *aber,* ſignifying the *mouth of a river,* pervades all the Celtic dialects, and differs almoſt nothing from the *Chabar* of the Eaſt.

From the ſame word we have the Greek υπερ, and γεφυρα, a *bridge*. Alſo the Lat. *ſuper, ſupra,* with all their connections. Upon the whole, hardly any particle has pervaded a greater number of dialects, both in Europe and Aſia.

Lee] Over all the North of Scotland they pronounce this word *ley,* which comes very near the Greek λειος, λευιων, λεια, &c.

VER. 3. *Gudewiſe*] Good, Scots *gude,* runs through all the Northern dialects. Its primitive is found in the old Perſian language, where it is *gath,* good. It is the root of the Greek αγαθος, good.

Wiſe] Of all the etymologies of this word, none ſeem to me more plauſible than that which refers it to the very word *chevah*. It is only changing the letter *heth* into *w,* and throwing away the *he* at the end; but the profound etymologiſts will reject this derivation, were it for no other reaſon but becauſe it is obvious.

Kaiu, Kaio] Theſe words are originally Perſian. *Kai,* or *Hei,* was a title given to a dynaſty of their Kings. Hence the

the Princes of that family were called *Kaianides*, which signifies the *splendid*, or *illustrious*. The word *hai*, *hei*, signifies *fulgur*, a flash of lightning. Hebr. *kai*, or *kei*, ustio, adustio; Gr. καιω, uro. From the same root the Latin prænomen *Caius*, borrowed, I suppose, from the Etruscans, a colony of Lydians, which last had it from their neighbours the *Medes*.

'γεραω] From γαω, gigno, which last from γεα, Terra, it being the opinion of the ancient uncivilized Greeks, that the original men sprung from the earth, according to the doctrine of Moschus, Democritus, and Epicurus, which was introduced afterwards, and formed upon the same opinion. The radical term is the Hebr. *gia*, vallis.

Gaudeo is, I believe, deduced from the Hebrew *gaah*, superbire; whence *gavah*, exultatio, which produces the Gr. γαω and the Lat. *gaudeo*, originally *gaveo*. The Scots word *gaff*, to laugh immoderately, belongs to the same family. They seem to be originally *onomatopæas*, formed in allusion to the sound of the human voice in an extasy of joy.

VER. 4. *Ludge*] Celt. *Lug*, *Log*, a place; whence Lat. *Locus*, and the Scot. *Logie*, the name of several villages. Hence also *Kil-logie*.

VER. 5. *Night*] This word, in various forms, pervades all the Northern dialects. With a small variation, we have Lat. *nox*, *noct*; Gr. νυξ; Hebr. Chad. Syr. *nuch*, quievit, requievit.

Wat] Pers. *ab*, *av*, *aw*, a river; the very same with the Celtic word *av*, signifying the same thing. Of *au* and *phrat*, the Greeks made Ευφρατης, Euphrates.

VER. 6. *Ingle*] The origin of this word is very obscure. In many places of Scotland they have no other fuel but peats, furze, broom, heath, and brushwood. Fires consisting of such materials must be fed by continual supplies, which they

L. 2   call

call *beeting*. The Welch vocable *inghilſt* ſignifies *feeding*; this I take to be the origin of the word *ingle*, alluding to the conſtant *feeding* of the fire. In like manner, Iſl. *elldur* is fire; *ellde*, to boil with fire; both from *el, ool, ela*, to feed.

Ver. 7. *Dochter's*] This word is purely Perſian, as is generally known.

Ver. 8. *Cadgily*] The word *cadge* is probably derived from the Sclavonian *chodge*, to trudge on foot; whence, too, our *ſcadgy*, a little wench, who does the dirty work in a farmer's kitchen. The word *cadgy*, in the preſent caſe, ſhould, I think, be written *cagy*, or *cagie*, which would agree better with the pronounciation. It imports *merry, chearful, jovial*, and is, I believe, an abbreviation of the old French word *cagedler*, the ſame with *cajoler*, to cajole, flatter, cox.

STANZA II.

Ver. 5. *Canty*] From Lat. *canto, cano*. Hebr. *kanah, canna*, calamus, arundo, plainly alludes to playing on inſtruments made of reeds, the reed being the firſt ſubſtance uſed for wind muſic. The Hebrew *chanah*, among other ſignifications, denotes *to ſing, to ſay, to ſpeak to, to teſtify, to atteſt*. The Greek ἀιδω, in ancient times, implied both to *ſing* and to *ſpeak*. By comparing theſe two ideas, it appears that the ancients uttered their words with a *canting* tone of voice, or in the recitative ſtile. From this circumſtance the orations of the Greeks and Romans may poſſibly have derived ſome part of that influence, which we ſtill admire, but have never ſeen.

Ver. 6. *Ken*] This is another word of Perſian extraction. In that language it denotes a learned intelligent man, eſpecially in the Laws of Zerduſht. Hence all the deſcendants of that word in Greek, Latin, Gothic, &c

STANZA

STANZA III.

VER. 2. *Daddy*] This word occurs, with little variation, in many different languages; *ab, ap, av-us, at, atta, tat, dad*, &c. and are all mere onomatopæas, fabricated from the early prattle of infants. The sound is formed by an application of the point of the tongue to the roof of the mouth, one of the most natural efforts of the organs of speech. It was probably caught by mothers and nurses, and by them applied to intimate the idea of *father*. This process was natural. The first articulate sound enounced by the child was appropriated to the idea of *father*, he being deemed superior in dignity to the other parent.

Di] Mentioned in the notes on the preceding word, signifies *bright, luminous, splendid, glorious*. It occurs in many of the Eastern dialects, and from thence probably found its way into the West. Persian *div*, a genius, whence Eol. Διβος, Lat. *divus*, Hebr. *zui*, splendor; Lat. *diu*, in the day-time; Gr. Δις, Jupiter, originally the *Sun*; Διος, divinus, and so forth.

This word makes the first part of Διονυσος, the Greek name of Bacchus, a word which has been strangely garbled by etymologists. In reality, *dio* signifies *bright*, and *nasia*, princeps. The Eolians changed *a* into *v*. Hence Dionysius will signify the *bright Prince*, or the *Prince of Light*, i. e. the Sun, who was indeed the original Bacchus of the Greeks, and Osiris of the Egyptians.

VER. 6. *Dyke*] Heb. *deik*, munitio, propugnaculum; Gr. τειχος. Hence all the progeny of that word throughout the Greek and Gothic dialects. Hence, too, the Gr. δεικω, δεικνυμι, *ostendo*, to point out, as from the top of a bulwark, fort, or tower. This word may be compared with the Lat. *specula, speculor*, to view from a watch-tower. In ancient

times

times it was the practice to erect watch-towers, or eminences, round the frontiers of a country, and in thefe to place a man, whofe bufinefs it was to *look out*, and, upon the approach of an enemy, to alarm the country by lighting up fires. Hence the *churim*, vigiles, Hebr. Chald. alluding to the kindling up *fires*; the Gr. φρυροι, from the fame idea; the Lat. *fpeculatores*, and the Scandinavian *gokefmen*.

VER. 7. *Clead*] To this family belong the Gr. κλωθω, neo, and Κλωθω, the eldeft of the *Deflinies*.

Braw] From *brage*, mentioned in the Note on this word, we have the Engl. *brag, braggodocio*, importing originally *loud-talking*. The Perfian word *brag* fignifies *fhining*, *fparkling*, and might be metaphorically applied to denote a perfon of *fhining* talents, which exactly fuits the Scandinavian *brage*.

Ladylike] *Lady*, compounded of Goth. *lhaif*, bread, and *dien*, to ferve, becaufe the miftrefs of the family ufed to diftri-· bute the *bread* to the guefts and domeftics.

STANZA IV.

VER. 1. *Twa*] Scots *twa*, Engl. *two*, Belg. *twee*, Swed. *twa*, Dan. *tœ*, Sax. *twa*, *twy*, Pal. *dwa*, Ruf. *twa*, Lat. *duo*, Gr. δυω, Welch *duy*, Ger. *zwan*, Perf. *do*, Beng. *dio*, Malay *duo*.

VER. 2 *Wee*] Little. This word bids fair for being the root of the Greek υιος, a fon. Hence, too, we have the Spanifh *hijo*, fignifying the fame thing. This is one of the many Gothic terms ftill fubfifting in the Spanifh tongue. Their etymologifts tell us, that the word *hidolgo*, which, in their language, fignifies a *gentleman*, is compounded of *hijo* and

and *algo*, i. e. *the son of something*. I believe they are mistaken. The word is made up of the two Gothic terms *hijo* and *idelg*, or *idolg*, which last, in that language, signifies a *gentleman*. A. S. *adel athæling*, nobly born.

Cock] The Celtic word *kok* signifies *red*; whence Greek κοκκος, and Latin *coccus*, purple. Perhaps this bird was so denominated from the *red colour* of his *crest*, or *comb*. Be that as it may, the creature is a native of Media, and therefore cannot endure the cold of these northern regions, without suffering very severely.

VER. 3. *Shot*] The root is the Scythian *sket*, an *arrow*. Perhaps it may not be amiss to enquire somewhat minutely into the origin and connections of this word, for reasons which will appear by and by. I shall not pretend to trace it through the Gothic dialects, all which it pervades, with little alteration of sound or signification. From the numerous cognates of this term, I shall single out the word *skeit*, or *skout*, which is nothing else but a modification of the original vocable. The present meaning of this word is universally known; but, I believe, few are acquainted with its original and primary acceptation.

The Celtic or Gaelic word *scuta* denotes a *vagabond*, a *restless wanderer, one perpetually roving about, without settling in any particular place, or fixed habitation*. From this definition it plainly appears, that it is of the same family with the word *scout*, mentioned above. This radical term, with the definition annexed, I owe to the translator of Ossian's Poems; and it enables me to ascertain the original import of two *names*, which have greatly embarrassed a multitude of critics, of different ages and countries. This word *scuta* is, beyond all doubt, the original of the Greek Σκυθα, Scytha, a *Scythian*. The sound and signification of the Celtic and

Greek

Greek word fix the analogy to a demonstration. It was, no doubt, applied to the Scythians, with a particular view to exhibit the roving, restless disposition of those people, who inhabited all the Northern regions of Asia and Europe. Analagous to this idea, the Persians called the same people Σακαι, Bacæ. Herod. l. 7. cap. 64. ιſ· Περσαι παντας της Συθας καλεσι Σακα. ; "Now the Persians call all the *Scythians*, *Sacæ*." The Persian word *ſack* is plainly a cognate of the Hebrew *ſhakak*, discurrere, discursitare, &c. The monosyllable root of the word is *ſhak*, or *ſheik*, and alludes to the very same restless, wandering disposition, that the word *ſcuta* does in the Celtic. Both the .κ..α: of the Greeks, and the *Sacæ* of the Persians, were terms of reproach, imposed by hostile neighbours; and, of course, were never adopted by the Scythians themselves, who always assumed a more honourable denomination.

From the same word *ſcuta*, and for the same reason, was derived the opprobrious name *Scot;* a name detested by the Aborigines of the country, who always call themselves by the Gentile appellation, *Albanich*. During the lower ages of the Roman Empire, the Aboriginous Britons, whom the Romans, upon their first invasion, had forced to take shelter among the fastnesses of the mountains, gradually recovered their courage, and, sallying from their strong holds, harrassed the Romans, and Provincial Britons, without distinction. As these people were perpetually roving about, and distressing the Province by desultory wars, the Provincial Britons, out of spite, branded them with the infamous epithet of *ſcuta*, in allusion to their wandering migratory course of life. The Romans soon caught the term from the Britons, and turned the word into *Scotti*, or *Scoti*.

In confirmation of this etymon, it may be observed, that, not many years ago, the Scots borderers used to call themselves

selves *scuytes*, and *skytes*, as we learn from Cambden. Indeed, less than a century ago, the term was current in the North of Scotland. The Saxon-Scots readily adopted this name, being ignorant of the original import of it; but the Scoto-Brigantes, or Highlanders, have always deemed it a term of reproach, and, consequently, still retain their original denomination, *Albanich*.

From the same word *Saca*, or *Sak*, explained above, the Saxons who settled in the North of Germany seem to have derived their name. They were probably a colony of Scythian emigrants, who settled in that country, and brought with them the Gentile name *Sak*, which had become the general denomination of these tribes of Scythians who lived nearest the frontiers of Media, and the other Provinces of the Persian Empire. Certainly the etymon assigned by Verstegan, Sir William Temple, and others, who tell us, that it is derived from *seaxen*, or *seaxes*, is highly improbable. These *seaxen*, or *seaxes*, were weapons much used by the Saxons. They were crooked after the fashion of a scythe, with the edge on the contrary or outward side. The plural, formed by *n*, instead of *s*, made *Seaxon*, which (says Verstegan, p. 21.) the Latins turned into *Saxons*.

VER. 4. *Bent*] This species of grass is seldom produced in marshy grounds. It appears in greatest plenty on any sandy hillocks, especially on sandy grounds lying on the sea-shore, which we call *links*. In Erse it is called *isnach*, which signifies *short, ill-grown*; Scot. *sitten*. Our ancestors used to twist ropes of it, for several purposes; hence, perhaps, it might be called *bent*, from Islandic *band*, Saxon *bandan*, vinculum.

M   STANZA

STANZA V.

Ver. 1. *Beggar*] To beg, to ask alms; from the Goth. *bidgan*, Isl. *bid*, Sax. *biddan*, to pray; whence *to bid beads*. Perhaps it may have originated from the practice of beggars, who use to pray for alms. The Hebr. *bag* signifies *meat*, and is, perhaps, a cognate of this term.

Ver. 2. *Strae*] There is an obvious analogy between this word and the Gr. ϛρωω, ϛρονυυμι; Lat. *strao*, *sterno*, to straw, to spread, to level. In this last sense, they seem to coincide with the word *strath*, (a level country, lying between two ridges of mountains) so common in all the Celtic dialects. *Strath* and *straith* are true Celtic words, a valley lying along a river. Vide Bullet, Dict. Celt. in *Strat* and *Strah*. To the same tribe belong Gr. ϛρατος, ϛραπα, ϛρατοπεδον, &c. These words were appropriated by the Greeks to signify a *camp*, an *army*, an *encampment*, &c. because the original mode was to chuse large level plains for encampments. For the same reason, the word *camp*, from the Lat. *campus*, a *plain*, is used by the French, Spaniards, Italians, and English, to denote the same idea.

The Latin word *sterno* signifies *to make a bed*, which was done by shaking, arranging, and levelling the *straw*; whence appears the relation of the ideas. Both Greeks and Latins call a bed-stead *torus*, because it was formed of *thongs of a bull's hide*, employed in the same manner as we now do *cords*. Thus Ossian often mentions the binding of prisoners with *thongs*. We learn, too, that in that Poet's time, thongs of leather were used aboard of ships for ropes. The Chald. *thor* is a *bull*; whence the ταυρος of the Greeks, and the *taurus* of the Latins. From these two ideas of *straw*, and *thongs of undressed leather*, we may infer, that the ancients of every rank slept not more softly than our peasants do at present.

Ver.

VER. 5. *Koffers*] Ifl. *kofe*, domuncula; *kofa*, cave.1, conclave. Here again we may recur to the Hebrew *kaph*, *cavum*, *vola*, *manus*, &c. Hence, too, we have the vulgar term *coft*, inftead of *bought*, i. e. *coffed*, put into my *coffer*.

Kifts] The root of this word is the Hebrew *kis*, loculus, marfupium, crumena.

STANZA VI.

VER. 2. *Kirn*] To the Author's numerous collections on the etymology of this word, we may add, that, agreeably to his idea, the Hebr. *geor* fignifies *eoire*, *convenire*, in the fame fenfe that the Latins fay, *in circulum venire*. I cannot difmifs this word without venturing a few ftrictures on the very different ideas affixed to it.

Gur, a verb, fignifies, among other things, to *fear*, to be *afraid*, to *dread*. *Gur*, a fubftantive-noun, imports a *ftranger*, an *incomer*, a *fojourner*. From the connection of thefe two ideas, we are led to infer the inhofpitable character of the ancients towards people of a foreign tribe, or clan, who refided among them. Their hofpitality to travellers, or paffengers, was indeed almoft unbounded; but with refpect to foreigners who fettled in their country, the cafe feems to have been widely different, as it ftill is in many places of the diftant Highlands: Hence, I fuppofe, the many injunctions we meet with in fcripture, inculcating beneficence and tendernefs towards ftrangers.

From *magor*, or *megor*, a compound of this word, we have *Mægara*, the name of one of the furies of hell, importing terror, difmay, &c.

From another compound of the word *magur*, *habitatio*, *commoratio*, we have the Greek μεγαρον, *domus*, *domicilium*, any large repofitory, or magazine; a word very common

common in Homer. From *Megurah* we have *Megara*, a city of Greece, mid-way between Athens and Corinth. *Garuth*, hospitium, is the very same with the Celtic *ghwarth*, a fort or castle. The same word produced the Persian *ghert, guerd*, a city, from which we have a numerous family of descendants in all the Gothic dialects. This word is likewise the parent of the Lat. *migro*, to remove; or, as we say in Scotland, to *flit*.

In the notes upon this word, which indeed shew a vast extent of etymological learning, the Author deduces the Greek αγορα, from the the primitive *gur :* To me it seems rather to be formed from the prefect. med. of the verb αγειρω, congrego, which is derived from the Hebrew *ager*, collegit, congessit.

Ver. 2. *Butt*] This word, with all its numerous progeny, was imported from Persia, where it appears nearly in the same form, *bad, bod, bud*, signifying, in that language, a *house*, a *dwelling*, an *abode*, the very same with the German and Scandinavian word in question. It is indeed the Hebr. *beth, beith*; Chald. *bith*; Arab. *bait*; Egypt. *but*. In Egypt, the place into which the initiated were put was called by this name. See Hesych. in voce. Also, βυτις, βωτις, and, without the Greek termination *but, bot*, was a kind of ship, resembling a floating-house or *booth*. From the same word we have the Greek κιβωτις, a wooden ark. Comp. of the Hebrew *geb*, gibbus, and *bot*. This word might be traced through a multitude of languages, and was, no doubt, a primæval term.

Ver. 4. *Ben*] To the numerous etymologies of this word traced by the Author, I shall presume to add one more, which will lead us back to the same original with *but*, of which it is the opposite. In the Chald. we find the word *benin, benina*, Ezr. v. 4. signifies ædificium, a house, a dwelling, from the Hebr. *bana*, ædificavit. From *benin* we may, without

out any violence, deduce the word *ben*, in the fame manner we do *butt* from *beth*.

STANZA VII.

VER. 8. *Bann'd*] This is another word of Perfian extraction. In that language the word *bend* fignifies a *chain*, and metaphorically an *obftacle*, a *barrier*, a *wall*.

STANZA VIII.

VER. 4. *Frae*] The fame nearly with the Gr. παρα. The radix is the Hebr. *pharad*, or *phrad*, feparavit, fejunxit. The root is *phar*, *phara*; or, without the point, *phra*. It is certainly connected with our words *far*, *frae*. Of this word *phar*, and Chald. *bara*, is formed the Greek Βαρβαρος, a Barbarian. In the oriental dialects it figuified *agreftis*, *rufticus*, a peafant; what idea the Greeks annexed to its derivative, is too well known to need to be mentioned.

The Author has fomewhere obferved, that there is certainly a very ftrict connection among the particles of almoft all languages. This obfervation is founded on fact; and I may add, that the not underftanding the nature, relations, fignification, and original import of thefe feemingly unimportant terms, has occafioned not only great uncertainty, but numberlefs blunders, in tranflating the ancient languages into modern tongues. The Greek language, in particular, lofes a confiderable part of its beauty, elegance, variety, and energy, when the adverbial particles, with which it is replete, are not thoroughly comprehended. An exact tranflation of thefe fmall words, in appearance infignificant, would throw new light not only on Homer and
Hefiod,

Hesiod, but even on poets of a much posterior date. Particles, which are generally treated as mere expletives, would often be found energetically significant. It is, however, altogether impossible to succeed in this attempt, without a competent skill in the Hebrew, Chaldean, Syrian, Arabic, Persian, Phœnician, Gothic, and Celtic languages. Such an extensive acquaintance with languages is, it is true, seldom to be found in one and the same person. I shall here take the liberty to mention a few of the most familiar of these particles, one or other of which occurs in almost every line of Homer, and which, I am persuaded, are generally misunderstood. Such are δη, φα, μεν, ην, μαν, μα, τοι, γε, οχ, γεν, αρα, ρα. All these particles are truly significant, and, if properly explained, would add considerable energy to the clauses in which they stand; but this disquisition must be left to the learned Philologers of the Universities.

VER. 7. *Laith*] The Author adduces very plausible arguments to prove, that the Greek word ελ.γος is derived from *laith*. I shall, however, adduce another etymology, and leave the choice to the judgment of the reader. In the Hebr. and Chald. we have the word *cheleg*, plur. *chelegim*; or, as some pronounce them, *oleg*, plur. *olegim*, *lisping*, *stammering*. In ancient times, ελεγος signified the same with θρηνος, lamentation. Those who lament use a whining tone of voice; which circumstance, perhaps, gave birth to the word.

STANZA IX.

VER. 7. *Town*] To the Author's quotation from Tacitus, may be added another from Cæsar de Bel. Gal. l. 5. cap. 21.

STANZA

STANZA X.

VER. 7. *Ca'*] Few words pass through more languages, and with less variation than this. Its root is the Hebrew *kol*, vox. Its cognates and derivatives spread themselves through the Arabic, Syrian, Chaldean, Persian, Greek, Latin, and Gothic, and are a striking instance of the universality of the primæval language.

It has been observed, in the course of these Notes, that the German and Scandinavian tongues abound with vocables of the same sound and signification. There are only two ways of accounting for this appearance: First, by supposing that these coincident terms were parts of the universal original language spoken by Noah and his family on the plains of Shinar, and preserved after the confusion of tongues at Babel: Or, secondly, by granting, that Colonies emigrated from the neighbourhood of Media and Persia, and at last settled in Germany and Scandinavia. Perhaps it might be owing to both causes. Without entering into a minute discussion of this point, which the bounds I have prescribed myself will not permit, I shall only observe, that the Median and Armenian tongues were different dialects of the same language. The Armenians, Syrians, Chaldeans, resembled one another in *features*, *language*, and *manners*. Again, the Phrygian and Armenian tongues bore so near a resemblance, that many have thought the former were descended from the latter. The Thracians and Phrygians are said to have been the same people, and therefore spake the same language. The Thracians and Getæ likewise spoke only different dialects of the same tongue. The latter spread themselves far and wide towards the West and North; probably they over-ran a considerable

part

part of Germany, and forced their way into Scandinavia. Some have thought that the Goths and Getæ were the same people. This, however, is a vulgar mistake, arising from the ignorance of the historians of the lower ages of the Roman Empire. If the links of this chain shall happen to be firmly connected, we need not be surprised at finding a great number of words pervade all the dialects spoken by these different and very distant nations.

CHRIST's

CHRIST's KIRK

ON THE

GREEN.

TO THE READER.

IN the Preface and Notes to the *Gaberlunzie-man*, I have endeavoured to make my Readers acquainted with the true system of rational Etymology, which consists in deriving the words of every language from the radical sounds of the first, or original tongue, as it was spoken by Noah and the builders of Babel. Many of these are preserved in the several dialects now in use over this globe, and every day brings more of those roots to our knowledge, as we grow better acquainted with the languages spoken by the several tribes of mankind. But the large collection of these radical terms will, one day, be laid before the Public, under the title of a *Scoto-Gothic Glossary*, if Heaven shall bestow health and leisure to complete the work.

Mean while, the Reader will be able to form some idea of my plan from the Notes on the preceding Poem; and, in the following observations, I shall confine myself to a more narrow circle of investigation, elucidating our ancient language from the later dialects of the primæval one, the *Gothic*, *Islandic*, *Teutonic*, and *Anglo-Saxon*.

To relieve the Reader from the tedious uniformity of etymological disquisition, I have interspersed some observations on the manners and customs of our ancestors, during the *middle ages*, which, I hope, will prove not unacceptable to the curious antiquarian.

Mr Ramsay has certainly departed very often from the orthography of Bannantyne's M. S. As I have no opportunity to consult that book, I have given such readings as appear to me most consonant to the phraseology of the sixteenth century.

The learned Bishop Gibson seems to have forgot that he was publishing a Scottish Poem—his orthography and idioms are quite English.

CHRIST's

CHRIST's KIRK ON THE GREEN*.

I.

WAS ne'er in Scotland heard or seen
   Sik dancing nor deray,
Nowther at Falkland on the green,
Or Peebles at the pley,
                              As

Chrift's Kirk on the Green] It is not eafy to affign the real name of the Author of this truly comic performance.— Tradition gives it to one of the James's, Kings of Scotland; and we find two of them named, James the Firft, and James the Fifth. In the *Evergreen*, it has the following note at the end, *Finis, quod K. James I.* Drummond's Hiftory of the James's, p. 16. fays, "This Prince was well fkilled in Latin "and Englifh poetry, as many of his verfes yet extant do tef- "tify." † While this hiftorian does not tell us what poetical performances

---

* Kirk-town of Leflie, near Falkland in Fife.

† Vide *Joan. Majoris Hift. Britan.* in vita *Jacob*, who mentions the firft two or three words of fome of thefe Poems abruptly, but furnifhes his Readers with no more; fo it would appear thefe are all now loft. But Major is a trivial writer, devoid of all tafte.

performances the King left, we cannot, with certainty, afcribe this little poem to him; efpecially as the language appears rather more modern than the year 1430. James I. was murdered Anno 1436. Maitland * talks as if many of James's writings were yet extant; but, in his ufual way, he only copies Drummond. Vide bottom of the preceding page.

Many different writers have faid that this Ballad was compofed by James V. and many arguments are advanced for this opinion; fuch as, the exact defcription of the manners and character of our Scottifh peafants, with which James V. was intimately acquainted, as he delighted in ftrolling about in difguife, among the lower people and farmers; in which excurfions he fometimes met with odd adventures, one of which he is faid to have made the fubject of his *Gaberlunzieman*, which we have, therefore, prefixed to *Chrift's Kirk on the Green;* and, indeed, the ftyle and ftrain of humour in both are perfectly fimilar.

The poetical talents of James V. made him known abroad; and it is to him the following verfes of Ariof. do refer † :

"Zerbino di bellezza, edi valore,
"Sopratutti Signori era eminenti," &c.

And, in the following Stanza, we find what country Zerbino belonged to:

"Pero, che data fine a la gran fefta,
"Il mio Zerbino in Scotia fe ritorno."

Ronfard, who accompanied James's Queen from France, and was his domeftic fervant, defcribes him thus:

"Ce

---

* Hiftory of Scotland, p. 613.
† Orlando Fur. Cant. 13. Stan. 8. 9.

" Ce Roy d'Efcoffe etoit en la fleur de fes ans,
" Ses cheveux non tondus, comme fin or luifans,
" Cordonnez et crefpez flottans deffus fa face,
" Et fur fon cou de lait luy donnoit bon grace.
" Son port etoit royal, fon regard vigoureux ;
" De vertus, et d'honneur, et de guerre amoureux;
" La douceur et la force illuftroit fon vifage,
" Si que Venus et Mars en avoient fait partage."

Maitland's Suffrage, concerning the tafte of James V. for poetry, were it of any avail, might be added; but he only copies fervilely from others.

There have been a good many different editions of this little Ballad, and the oldeft I have met with is one printed at Oxford in quarto *, and illuftrated with Notes by the learned Bifhop Gibfon, in which he has fhewn much knowledge of the ancient Northern languages. As the fpelling, however, of his edition is widely different from that ufed by the beft of the cotemporary authors, I have followed, in this one, the orthography of the collection called *The Evergreen,* but much corrected, as more truly correfponding to the Scottifh idiom and pronunciation. The Notes of the learned Bifhop are diftinguifhed from thofe of the Editor by the letter G.

In the edition by Bifhop Gibfon we find two entire ftanzas more than in that of Allan Ramfay, which, he fays, were copied from Bannantyne's M. S. Collection of Scottifh Poems, in Lord Hyndford's library, now in the Advocates library, to whom his Lordfhip prefented it, written in the year 1568. Thefe we have retained, as they are evidently in the fame ftyle and manner as the others, and even appear neceffary for connecting the ftory. They are alfo warranted by Gibfon's edition, being printed thirty-three years earlier than that of Ramfay.

There

* Anno 1691

There are several variations in the reading of these two editions, which we have marked in the Notes; but we have principally followed the spelling of Ramsay's edition corrected, the Bishop having often adopted not only the English orthography, but even the phrases of that language.

We have only to add, that if the little specimen now given of our ancient poetry shall prove acceptable to the real judges of good letters, and the public in general, it is designed to print a full collection of all the Scottish Poems which appeared before the seventeenth century, illustrated with Notes, in the manner of those that follow; in which undertaking we look for the kind assistance of all who love the language and antiquities of our country, and who wish to preserve the poems of our ancestors from oblivion.

" *Nobis pulchrum imprimis videtur, non pati occidere* " *quibus æternitas debeatur*," as Pliny the younger says, L. 5. Ep. 8.

STANZA I.

VER. 2. *Deray*] Jollity and merriment; *feasting* and *frolicking*, which are generally accompanied with riot and disorder. In this sense G. Douglas uses it * :

" Of the banket, and of the grete *deray*,
" And how Cupid inflames the lady gay."

And, speaking of the disorder in the enemy's camp, made by Nisus and Eurialus † :

" Behaldand al there sterage and *deray*."

Ruddiman

* Virgil, p. 35. l. 12. † Ibid, p. 288. l. 16.

Ruddiman derives the word from the French *defroyer*, which Pasquier explains, *tirer hors de voye, ou de roye*. Hence *arroy*, and our word *array*; and *difarroy, difarray*. From *defroyer* this critic also deduces the Scots word *royd*, or *royet*, romping, frolicksome; taking away the first syllable, as in *skirmish*, from *escarmouche*; *sample*, for *example*; *uncle*, from *avunculus*; *spittal*, for *hospital*.

Thus far Mr Ruddiman, who, had he been better acquainted with the Northern languages, would have known that the origin of this word is of much higher antiquity than the old French he quotes. *Rud*, in the Gothic, signifies *line*, or *order*. Thus, in one of their old books *, *Then kunungr the hawær kuninglikt wald met arfde rad*, That King who succeeds according to the *line* of succession. Islandic *raud* and *rada*, to put in order; Saxon, *na der radt*, according to order. In the Scythian dialects we find this ancient word varied by many different terminations. Alam. *ruava*; Angl. *row*; and the Scots, who, we shall often find, retain the ancient Gothic pronounciation, say, *raw*; Welsh *rigwun*; Fenn. *riwi*; Ital. *riga*. Hence the French *raye*, and, by inserting an *n*, *rang*, whence we form *rank*; Belg. *rege*, *rijge*, whence the Scottish *rig*, a ridge of corn, from its streightness and regularity. In Ulphila we find, *Rathjan* †. *garathanu sind alla izwara tagla haubidis*, Numbered are all the hairs of your heads ‡. In Swed. *rakna*, to reckon or number; Lat. *ratio*.

As the ancients generally used counters in summing up their accompts, disposed in rows, *rad* is the common phrase on such occasions in the dialects of the North. Hence *Attradur* is he who

---

* Kon. Styr. p. 24. apud Ihre, Lex. in Rud.
† Joh. vi. 10.   ‡ Matth. x. 30.

who hath attained to the *eight line*, *i. e.* fourscore years; *Nirædur*, a man ninety years old ; *Tha var Haraldur Konung aatradur at aldoi*, King Harald was then eighty years old *. And in the Islandic bible †, *Abram hafdi sex um attræt*, Abram was eighty-six years old.

VER. 4. *Peebles at the pley*] In the old writers we find this word used in several senses. To *pley* is to *plead*, carry on a law suit ; Belg. *pleyten*. In Welsh we find the word *pleidio*, to act as advocate for any. Vide Jun. in *Plead*. Douglas, Virg. p. 73.

" ──── Follow our chance bot *pleys*."
i. e. Without disputing.

And p. 445.

" The auld debate of *pley*, or controversy."

P. 3. 34. *But pleid*, Without controversy. Now, as our ancestors always resorted to the courts of law, armed and attended by their vassals and dependents, it often happened that their differences were decided by sharper weapons than lawyers tongues. Hence the A. S. *plegan*, to strike, to wound in war ; *plega-gares*, the play of spears. Cædmon, 45. 11. *Heard hand-plega*, The hard play of hands. Vide Lye, Lex. Sax. in *Plega*. Hence Spelman in Archeol. derives *plea* from *pleah*, damnum, periculum. *Play*, or *pley*, was hence used to denote tilts and tournaments, as at these meetings it was very frequent with the knights to give proof of their address and valour in mock engagements, which, however, often terminated in blood. The ladies always were present at such meetings, and gave the prizes.

──── " of

* Olaf Trygg. Saga. Part. I. p. 11.   † Gen. xviii.

As was of wooers as I ween
At Chryſt's Kirk on a day;
There came owr Kittys waſhen clean,
In new kyrtills of gray,
    Fow gay that day.

II.

 ―――" of wit and arms, while both contend
 " To win her grace, whom all commend." *Milton.*

The town of Peebles was, in ancient times, a place of ſome note. Here was a conſiderable Priory; and, being the largeſt town in that diſtrict of Scotland, it is likely that frequent and numerous meetings were held here. The open plains, too, round this city, made it a very proper place for tournaments, and other warlike exerciſes. *Pley,* the cuſtomary meeting. Iſl. *plaga,* Goth. *plæga,* ſolere, alſo exercere. It is probable one of theſe exerciſes gave riſe to a Scottiſh Poem ſimilar to this, entitled *Peebles on the Play,* ſaid to be preſerved by the Reverend Dr Percy of Carliſle.

VER. 5. *Ween*] Suppoſe; think. Sax. *wenan,* opinari; Goth. *wenian,* Gibſon. In the Alemanic it is *wanen.* The root is in the Gothic *wenian.* Thus Ulphila, Luke iii. 15. *At weniandein than allai managein,* All the people thinking. Confer Jun. Lex. Ulphil. *Wende,* in Chaucer, to think or conſider. Tr. lib. 3. 1547.

 " And in his thought gan up and down to *wende.*"

VER. 7. *Kittys*] Either from *Kate, Katie,* the common diminutive of Catherine; or from their playfulneſs as *kittens,* or Scot. *kitlings,* young cats.

VER. 8. *Kirtle*] Mantle. Iſl. *kiortell.* Of old we find the ſame term applied to the gowns worn by the men.

            Thus

II.

To danfs thir damyfells them dight,
Thir laffes light of laits;
Thir gluvis war of the raffal right,
Thir fhoon war o' the ftraits.

Thir

Thus Franco-Goth. *Ung aultre lui veftira un kyrtel du rouge tartarin.* Vide Cange, Gloff. Lat. vol. 4. p. 737.

STANZA II.

VER. 1. *Dight*] Prepared, or made them ready. Sax. *Dightan*, parare, inftruere; vox Chaucero ufitatiffima. Thus, *dighteth* his dinner. To bed thou wold be *dight*. His inftruments wold be *dight*.—Gibfon.

May it not rather be derived from *deccan*? Sax. Metaphor. *Excolere*, *ornare*. Alam. *Thecan*. Perhaps, too, we are hence to derive the word *deck* of a fhip. Mr Ruddiman (Gloff. to Bifhop Douglas) obferves, that in Chefhire the word *dight* is ufed in the oppofite fenfe to foul or dirty; but this is only provincial, like many other corruptions.

VER. 2. *Laits*] If this word is rightly copied from the M. S. it may fignify nimble, or light-footed. Goth. *laiftjan*, fequi. Vide Jun. Gloff. Ulph. in voce. Thus Luke ix. v. 59. *Laiftci mik*, Follow me. Theotis. Gloff. Kalepodia. *leift*. Dan. *left*; Angl. *laft*, on which the fhoe is formed. Hence Sax. *fotleft*, veftigium, footftep. Vide Pf. lxxxvi. v. 19.

VER.

Thir kirtles were of Lincome light,
Weel preft wi' mony plaits;
They were fae fkych, whan men them nicht,
They fqueil'd like ony gaits,
Fu' loud that day.

III.

VER. 3. *Gluvis*] So our anceftors fpelled *gloves*. Sax. *glofes*. Jun. in Etymol. obferves, that in Danifh they are called *haand-kloffuer*, from *haand* and *kloffue*, to fplit or divide, which gives the true idea of the word *glove*. Hence *glofar, gloar, glofe, glove*.

Raffal] I don't well underftand the meaning of this word; but, from analogy, it muft fignify gloves of rough leather. Celt. *craf*, nails of the fingers—a file—every thing that fcratches. Hence fkins dreffed in a rough manner, with coarfe inftruments, and not fmoothed. Confer Bullet in V. *Craf*.

VER. 4. *Straits*] Quære, Is this what we now call Morocco leather, from the Straits of Gibraltar?

VER. 5. *Lincome*] Is this rightly copied from the M. S.?

VER. 6. *Plaits*] Folds. Douglas, p. 298. v. 4.

" And he his hand *plait* on the wound in hye."

Plait, nectere, contexere; Gr. πλεκειν; A. S. *plett, pletta*, a fheep-fold, they being of old made of wicker work. The Scots called them *faulds*, for the fame reafon, and the Englifh *folds*.

VER. 7. *Skygh*] Shy. *Skygg bafta*, à fhy horfe.—Jun.

VER. 8. *Squeil'd*] Shrieked. Sueo-Goth. *fqwallra*, blaterare; *fqwæla*, incondite vociferare; Angl. *fqueak, fqueal*. Douglas, of cattle, p. 254. 40.

" Bayth

" Bayth *squeil* and low."

And p. 248. 36.

" With loud voce *squeland*."

It is used metaphorically to accuse; *Sqwallra uppa en*, aliquem accusare; Vide Ihre Lex. Sueo-Goth. in *Sqwallra.* *Sqwalungar*, crying children, squaling brats. Suio-Goth. *skall*, found; Alam. *scall*; Germ. *schall*. " Usurpa- " tur a nobis," says the learned Ihre, " vel pro sonitu for- " tiori in genere, vel etiam in specie, quum multitudo, edito " clamore, feras in casses propellit." Hence *skallalæghe*, society of hunters; *skalra*, to cry out; *skalla*, to bark or howl as a dog. Hence *skælla*, a small bell, which was hung to the robes of men in power, that the passengers might make way for them. Chron. Ryth. Min. in Præfat.

" Kunde han danza, springa ok hoppa,
" Han skulle jw hafwa skallo, och forgylta klocka."

" If he only could dance and hop gracefully, he had immediate- " ly gilded bells given him." Confer Ihre in *Skælla*. The old French Romance *De la Viollette*, ap. Cange in *Mantum*, describing a rich robe:

" Et ot a chascune flourette,
" Attachie une campanette.
" Dedans si que rien n'en paroit,
" Et si tres doulcement sonnoit,
" Quant an mantel frapoit le vent."

The antiquity of this ornament appears from the sacerdotal robes of the Jewish priests, and those used by other nations. Apul. Met. Lib. 10. Et pictilibus balthæis, et tintinnabulis perargutis exornatum. Adde Eccard. ad LL. Salic. p. 151. where he observes, that the Ital. *squilla* is of the Gothic fami- ly. In the Latin of the middle ages we have *schilla—*
esquilla;

III.

Of a' thir maidens, myld as meid,
Was nane fae jimp as Gillie;
As ony rofe her rude was red,
Her lyre was lyke the lillie:
But

efquilla, and *fquillare*, for *fonare*. It was alfo the cuftom to hang bells to the necks of cattle, that they might be more eafily found in the woods: And hence the penalty in the Salic Law, cap. 29. againft him, Qui fkellam de caballis furaverit. Confer Cange in *Tintinnabulum*.

VER. 8. *Gaits*] Goats. Sax. *geit, gat*; Ifl. *geit*, capra; Goth. *gateins*, hædus.—Gib.

This is one of the many examples where the Scots have retained the orthography and pronunciation of the mother language, more exactly than the Englifh.

STANZA III.

VER. 1. *Meid*] Mead, hydromel, a favourite drink of our anceftors, and alfo of the Scandinavians, as we learn from Snorro, and all the Northern hiftorians. Mead and ale, called by them *ol*, were the conftant beverages ufed in their feafts; *Cujus frequentiffimus ufus eft in frigidis terris*, fays Olaus Magnus, lib. 13. cap. 21. where he has given us an account of the different methods they ufed in preparing that liquor, which may be of ufe to our modern brewers. Vide cap. 22. 23. 24. It is called by the Icelanders *miæd*;

Alam.

Fow zellow, zellow, was her heid,
 And fcho of luve fae filly,
Thocht a' hir kin had fworn hir deid;
 Scho wald hae nane but Willie,
    Alane that day.

IV.

Alam. *mede;* A. S. *medu, meodu;* Welfh, *meddeglyn,* hydromeli; Gr. μεδυ, vinum.

VER. 2. *Jimp*] Slender, handfome, G. *Gim, gimp;* complus, bellus, concinnus; Welfh, *gwymp;* Armor. *coant,* pulcher.

VER. 3. *Rude*] Blufh. Sax. *rudu;* Cimb. *rode, rubor.* Properly complection, the *verecundus color* of Horace, Epod. 17. Chaucer, Sir Topas; v. 13.

"His *rudde* is like fcarlet in graine."

Douglas, Virg.

"So that the *rude* did in her viffage glow."

Jun. Etymol. quotes from Jofephus, the ῥοδ'ανον τε σωματος; the rofeate colour of the fkin, which perfectly expreffes the *rude* of our Poet.

VER. 4. *Lyre*] Bifhop Gibfon derives this from the Cimb. *hlyre,* or the Sax. *hleare,* gena, maxilla, mentum, facies, vultus, quoting that of Chaucer:

"Saturn his *lere* was like the lede."

But the learned annotator is certainly miftaken; for it comes from A. S. *lire,* which fignifies (fays Lyc) Pulpan, quicquid carnofum eft, et nervofum in homine, ut *earflyre* nates, fcanclira, scanclira, sura. Thus it means in general *flesh*, as in Wallace's History, b. 7. c. 1.

"Burnt up bone and *lyre*."

And elsewhere:

" Through bone and *lyre*."

Douglas, Virg. p. 19. 35.

" Syne brocht flikerand sum gobbetis of *lyre*."

And p. 456. 1.

" Wyth platis full the altaris by and by,
" And gan do charge, and wourschip with fat *lyre*."

VER. 5. *Zellow*] Thus our ancestors used the z, though they always pronounced the words so spelled as if they had been written with the letter *y*. The reason seems to have been, that the *gh*, to which *y* has succeeded in later times, had been taken by ignorant transcribers for a z, as it bore some resemblance to it in the Saxon writing. This seems the more probable, as we find the Anglo-Saxon character still in use after the conquest; and, even under Edward the Third, the Monks blended Saxon letters with the Roman. See Mandeville's Travels, printed at London 1725, and Robert of Glocester's Chronicle in 1724, exactly after the original MSS. Hence, too, we must account for the changes we find in the names of many places. Thus, *Yetland* was the original name of the island which, from the above-mentioned mistake, came afterwards to be written *Zetland*, and which is now corrupted, by vulgar use, into its present form *Shetland*.

Though the z be used in the Gothic tongue, (Vide Ulphila's Gospels passim) yet it is not found in the Islandic alphabet, nor is it much used in the Sueo-Gothic; so that the learned Ihre calls it *Literam Suecis peregrinam*. The figure

IV.

Scho fkornit Jock and fkrapit at him,
 And murgeon'd him wi' mokks;
He wald hae luvit, fcho wald not lat him,
 For a' his zellow lokks;
          He

z much refembles the Saxon *g*, which the later Englifh have changed in moft words into *y*; as *geard, yeard; gea, yea; gear, year; geong, young*; and the Scots ftill more frequently, (as Ruddiman obferves) even where the Englifh retain *g*; as *yate*, for *gate; foryet*, for *forget*, &c. Junius has ranged all the words in Douglas's Virgil, which begin with *z*, under *g*. Vide his Gloff.

STANZA IV.

VER. 1. *Skrapit*] So Ramfay's edition. Bifhop Gibfon reads *fkripped*, which he explains, " Made a courtfie to him " in a mocking manner." " Vox deducenda videtur (adds he) per metathefin et fyncopen a Cimbr. *fkapraunade*, opprobrio vexabat. Bibl. Ifland. 1 Sam. 1. 6.

Perhaps this word may be, with more facility, derived from Sueo-Goth. *fkrapa*; A. S. *fcreope*, a fcraper; fcreopan, radære, fcalpere. Hence the faying, *Fa en fcrapa*, to be blamed or mocked. Perhaps our phrafe, *To fall into a fcrape*, may have originated from this. Shall we look here, too, for the root of the Latin *crepo, increpo*, with the *s* prefixed, as the Goths ufually do? Similar metaphor in the French, *Etriller* de paroles.

                We

CHRIST's KIRK ON THE GREEN.

We have further to obferve, that the Goth. *fkrap* properly fignifies *ufelefs fragments* of any thing, which we call *fcraps*. Hence metaphorically *a lazy ufelefs fellow*. Anfg. Saga cap. Ihre Lex. in *Skrap*, *Thu eft mefta heims fkripe*, Tu omnium bipedum ignaviffimus es. As fuch people are often vain-glorious, we have the verb *fkrappa*. Jactare fe, gloriari, *fkrappa vet fkryta*. Hence Lat. *crepare*, in the fame fenfe. *Skræp*, jactatio, oftentatio.

VER. 2. *Murgeon'd*] Made mouths at him, G. The A. S. *murcnung*, murmuratio, querela, querimonia ; Goth. and Ifl. *mogla*, murmurare.

VER. 3. *Luvid*] This may be underftood in the common acceptation of *loving*. But our anceftors ufed it for *praifing*. Thus Douglas, Virg. p. 455.

" How Eneas, glaid of his victory,
" *Lovit* the goddis, and can'them facrify."

Bruce's Life, p. 248.

" They *loved* God, and were full fain,
" And blyth that they efcaped fo."

Perhaps from the French *louer*, fays Ruddiman ; but this word is formed from Goth. *lof*, praife. The words, in that language, *loft*, *luft*, *lyfta*, all denote fomething *high* and *lofty*. *Lofwa*, laudare ; Ifland. *leiva*. In the Havamal, *Atqueld fkal dag*, *leiva konu tha kender, mæke er reindur, is tha yfer um killmer*, *i. e*. Praife the day when evening is come, a wife when you know her, a fword when you have tried it, and ice when you have paffed it. *Loftig*, laudable ; *lofurd*, commendation.

P VER.

He cherifh'd her, fcho bid gae chat him,
Scho compt him not twa clokkis,
Sae fchamefully his fchort goun fet him,
His legs war lyke twa rokkis,
   On rungs that day.
        V.

VER. 5. *Chat him*] To go about his bufinefs, G. Properly to take care of himfelf, and not attend to her, from the Gothic *fkota*, curare. Chron. Rython. apud Ibre, Lex. p. 619.

"Han wille thet intet *fkota*,
"Parum id penfi habebat."

Ifl. *fkeita*. Job 18. *Thes fem ecke fkeita um gud*, qui deum non curant. The fame learned and moft ingenious etymologift obferves the correfpondence of the Fr. *Il ne me chaut*, I care not; from the old *chaloir*. He adds, Credo noftrum a *fkot finus* factum, ut a *finus* fit *infinuare*, adeoq; propriè ufurpatum fuiffe de infantibus qui in finu portabantur, unde hodieq; *fkoting* dicitur tenellus, quem nondum de finu deponere licet. Hence applied to other things, *Skota fit ambele*, to look after his charge. Adde Douglas, p. 239. v. 30.

VER. 6. *Clokkis*] Beetles, fcarabæi, G. True, the beetle in the Scot. is *clok*; but perhaps it means here, fhe valued him no more than the *cluk* of a hen, which our anceftors pronounced *clok*, from the found the hen makes.

VER. 7. *Schort Goun*] Till the French taught us to wear our clothes fhort in the prefent fafhion, the gown, covering the knees, was univerfally worn both in England and Scotland. Hence Jun. derives it from γυνα pro γυατα, genua.
                  But

But the etymon is from the Welſh *gwn*, a gown or cloak, from *gunio*, fuere. In the *True Protraiture of Geoffrey Chaucer, the famous Engliſh poet, as it is deſcryved by Thomas Ocleve, who was his ſcholar*, and is generally put before the title-page in the old editions of Chaucer, we find him cloathed in the true Engliſh gown, cloſe gathered at the collar and wriſts, and flowing looſely down from the ſhoulders to the knees. The form of this garment we had from Germany; and it ſeems to have been imported by the Saxons, as it was worn all over Germany. Vide Spelman in *Guna*. The opulent had their gowns lined with ermine, and other rich furs; the poorer people with hare and ſheep ſkins. Boniface, Archbiſhop of Mentz, epiſt. 89. Gunnam de pellibus lutrarum factum fraternitati væſtrie miſi. Vinea Benedict, cap. 5. Senibus noſtris gunnas pelliceas tribuimus. Sometimes wrote *gonna*. Thus Gul. Major, apud Cange, in *Gonna*; Canonici ejuſdem eccleſiæ in gonnis ſuis. In old French *Gonne*. In the Romance of Guillaume del. Nez:

" Or feraigrè, fil me tollent ma *gonne*."

And ibid. apud Cange ubi ſup;

" Laiſſa le ſiecle, pour devenir prodhom,
" Et priſt la *gonne*, et le noir chaperon."

As *guna*, or *gown*, denoted the men's garment, the women's was called, in the barbarous Latin of the middle ages, *gunella*, becauſe made pretty near in the faſhion of the men's robe. Ital. *gonella*; Fr. *gotillon, cotillon*. Cluverius Germ. Ant. l. 1. c. 15. derives *gunam* a *gonaco*, quod Varro *majus ſagum* interpretatur, vocem Græcam eſſe ait. Hyſech. καυνακα, ςρωματα, ἡ επιβολαια ετιρομαλλα, ſtragula, altera parte villoſa. We ſhall, in another work, prove evidently, that numbers of the Greek words are formed from the Gothic, of which this is one, the robe itfelf being of Gothic, and not Greek invention. We find a Count of Angers firnamed *Grife-gonelle*, from his wearing a gown furred with that colour. Vide Cange Gloff. in *Grifeus* color. And we find an Epiftle of Pope John, folemnly addreffed to him, Goffrido *Grifia-gonellas cognominato*, nobilliffimo Andegavorum comiti. The men's gown is fometimes called *cappa*. Baldricus in Geft. Alberonis, ap. Cange, ubi fup. Clericali fe togo induit—et cappa de panno grifco fe fuper induit. Hence the faying of Henry IV. of France : "Je ne fuis q'un pauvre " here. Je n'ai que la *cappe* et l'efpée."

VER. 8. *Rokkis*] *Rock*, in Gothic and Iflandic, properly denotes a heap of any loofe things flung together. Thus *rock hoys*, a heap or rick of hay; and thus it is ftill ufed in Belg. Hence transferred to a heap of lint or wool put upon the ftick for fpinning. The tranfition was eafily made, when *rock* was ufed to denote the piece of wood to which the lint or wool was fixed. Thus the Chron. Ryth. apud Ihre Lex. in *Roak*, p. 496.

" Quinnor tager theras hæft ock harnijfk ifra,
" Ok monde them med *rockin* fla."
" *Women took the horfes and breaftplates from the men*,
" *And beat them with their* rocks."

Ifl. *rock*, and apud Kilian. Lex. Tuet. *rocken*, penfum colo aptare. See the learned Ihre, Lex. Sueo-Goth. in voce. Marefchall Obf. ad Verf. Angl. Sax. 4. Evangel. informs us, that in the times of Paganifm, the belt of Orion was, by the Scandinavians, called *Frygr rock*, colum deæ Fryggæ. Thus the girl here compares Jock's gown to an ill-fhaped heap of lint on the rock. Might not his ill-fhaped legs, if flender, &c. be compared to the rock or diftaff? Another Scottifh

CHRIST's KIRK ON THE GREEN. 117

tish Poem defcribes the legs like *barrow-trams*. Perhaps, too, *rock* may here be meant of the gown he wore, which looked as if it had been hung on a pole; for *rock* Goth. and A. S. *rocc*, fign. *toga*, veftis exterior; Al. *rokk*. In the barbarous Latin, *roccus*, *rochus*. Vide Cange Gloff. in voce. Gall. *rochet*. Whence we call the outer-garment of a fucking-child a *rochet*, or *rachet*, and the Englifh, putting *f* before, have formed their word *frock*; Gall. *froc*. Stadenius derives *rock* from *rauh*, rough, hairy. Ulphil. *rih*, as our anceftors firft were clothed in fkins, and after wool came to be ufed, they continued to line their gowns with furs of different kinds. The Finlanders ftill call a furred gown *roucka*, and the bed-coverings they ufe, made of fheep-fkins, are named *roucat*; whence our *rug*.

From this origin comes *rocklin*, the linen veftment worn by the priefts; the bifhops *rocket*. Thus Hiftor. Sigifmund. ap. Ihre Lex. vol. 2. p. 450. *Aflagges præftens hwita rocklin*, abrogatur facerdotis linea toga. This word was ufed in the fame fenfe by the ancient Latins, as we fee from Feftus; *Rica*, veftimentum quadratum, fimbriatum, purpureum, quo Flaminæ pro palliolo utebantur—Titinius. *Rica* et lana fucidei, alba veftitus. Our readers will find many learned and critical miftakes in the notes on this paffage, which is quite plain to thofe who know that it is a Gothic or Scythian term, as many more of the ancient Latin words are. Confer Jun. Etym. in *Rokette*; Spelm. in *Rocketum*.

VER. 9. *Rungs*] Round and long pieces of wood. Vox in ufu apud Anglos boreales, G.

Properly poles, or long ftaves like hunting poles, frequent in Douglas, and our old writers. Skinner fays the carpenters call thofe timbers in a fhip, which conftitute her floor, and are bolted to the keel, *rungs*.

STANZA

V.

Tam Lutar was thair minſtrel meet;
Gude Lord! how he cou'd lans!
He playt fae fchill, and fang fae fweet,
Quhyle Towſie took a tranſs.

Auld

STANZA V.

VER. 1. *Minſtrel*] This term was indiſcriminately applied to the harper, the fiddler, or the player on the bagpipe. Fr. *meneſtrier*. It appears to be derived from A. S. *minſter;* and thoſe called *minſtrells* were employed in the public worſhip of the cathedrals as ſingers, (vide Jun. in voce) in the ſame way the Welſh called muſicians *cler*, as employed in the ſame way. Thoſe minſtrels, during the middle ages, united the arts of poetry, inſtrumental and vocal muſic, their ſongs being always accompanied with the harp. Thus, too, our Poet repreſents his minſtrel, in ver. 3. below, as playing and ſinging. They ſeem to have been the genuine ſucceſſors of the ancient bards, who, under different names, were admired and honoured from the earlieſt ages among the Gauls, Britiſh, Iriſh, and Scandinavians; and, indeed, by all the firſt inhabitants of Europe, whether of Celtic or Gothic origin. It were eaſy to add many curious particulars concerning this once famed race of muſicians and poets; but we refer our Reader to the elegant diſſertation on the ancient Engliſh minſtrels, prefixed to the Reliques of Ancient Poetry, where we find it obſerved, that the light of the ſong (to uſe Oſſian's expreſſion) never aroſe without the harp. Douglas, Virg. 250. 18.

" Syne

"Syne the menſtrallis, ſingaris, and danſaris,
"About the kyndlit altaris."

Du Cange has collected a number of curious anecdotes concerning theſe minſtrells, voce *Miniſtelli*. The uſual theme of their ſongs we may learn from an old French romance, quoted by this lexicographer:

"Quiveut avoir des bons et des vaillans,
"Il doit aler ſouvent a la pluie et au champs,
"Et eſtre en la battaille, ainſi que fut Rolans,
"Les quatre fils Haimon, et Charlons li plus grans,
"Li dus Lions de Bourges, et Guion de Connans,
"Percival li Galois, Lancelot et Triſtans,
"Alixandres, Artus, Godefroy li Sachans,
"Dequoy cil menetriers font les nobles Romans."

VER. 2. *Lans*] To run or ſkip; metaphorically to dance. Arm. *Lanca*, jaculari, lanceam vibrare. The minſtrels, in general, could acquit themſelves as dancers, as well as ſingers and poets. Douglas, Virg. p. 297. 16.

——"Turnus *lanſand* lightlie over the landis,
"With ſpear in hand purſewis."——

Some think the phraſe *to launch a ſhip*, comes from this word. Vide Eſſay prefixed to Reliques of Ancient Poetry, p. 41. This ancient Celtic word has pervaded many dialects. Baſq. *lancza*; Gael. *langa*; Corn. *lancels*; Alam. *lanze*; Gr. λογχη; Hung. *lantſas*, a ſpearman. Hence Lat. *lanceare*, *lancinare*. Confer Voſſ. Etym. Lat. in *Lancea*.

VER. 4. *Tranſs*] The name of ſome foreign dance, perhaps then firſt uſed in Scotland, and oppoſed to *Lightfute*, a ſpecies of the *hayes*, or, as the Scots call it, *reel*, a *train*. Belg. *trein*, ingens eſſe clarûm numerus (ſays Jun.) qui
ductorem

Auld Light-fute thair he cou'd fore-leet,
And counterfittet Franfs ;
He held him as a man difcriet,
And up the Moreis-danfs
     He tuke that day.

VI.

ductorem fuum comitatur; une queue trainante, une traine de gens; of which train Towfie was the leader, or *choragus*, as in this manner the Morefco dances are ftill performed, which are mentioned below.

 VER. 5. *Fore-leet*] To outdo, G. This is an error; for *forlata*, Goth. fignifies to leave off, to defert. Job 4. 3. *Ho kan forlatat?* Quis illud derelinquere poterit? Ulphil. *traletan.* So Mark viii. 3. *Jabai fraleta ins laufqui thrans;* If I fend them away empty. The Iflanders write it *frilata*, and *fyrirlita.* Vide Snorro, vol. 1. p. 103. The prepofition *för*, generally indicates a bad acceptation. Thus *forhæda*, to contemn; and, where God is fpoken of, to blafpheme. *Forhala*, to delay; *forhægda*, to deftroy; *forhalla*, unjuftly to detain what is due to another. An hundred more examples might be given: Thus Towfie here *fore-leets*, leaves off and defpifes the dances of his own country, and betakes him to the French and Morefco tunes.

 VER. 7. *Up-tuke*] He took up; he began. Phrafis eft Cimbrica. Etenim tafia, tafia till, et tafia upp, ap. Iflandos fignificant *incipere*, ut, ogg drottins andetof ad vera med honum, cæpitq; fpiritus domini effe cum eo. Gib.

 Goth. *taga*, in general, to take. *Taga til lans*, to take on credit; *taga arf*, to take or fucceed to an inheritance; Ifl. *taka.* The great antiquity of this word may be feen in the
Latin

Latin *tagere*, and *tagax*, ap. Cicero. Qui lubenter capit,
rapax. Plaut. Milite:

" *Tetigit* calicem clanculum."

That is, ftole or *took* it. Hence *integer*, from whom nothing
is taken. *Taga* alfo fignifies *proficere*. *Han tager fik
wackert.* Pulchre proficit. He *takes* to it. Meric. Caufau-
bon. de Ling. Angl. Sax. p. 366. Ταω vel τακω, τἐ]ακα. Aor.
2. Partic. τἐ]αγων. Exponunt quidam τεινας, alii τιναζας,
alii deniq; λαβων, accipiens, prehendens, quos Steph. fequitur
—Certe. Tn imper. ex ταω—omnes exponunt λαβε. Cape.
Angl. take. It fignifies alfo *to choofe*. *Taka konung*, regem
eligere. Snorro, vol. 1. p. 65. *Taga lag*, legem accipere.

VER. 8. *Morris Dance*] Afric or Moorifh dance. A la
Morefca, It. Fr. *Morefque* : Hence corruptly *Morris dance*.
This kind was much ufed by our anceftors, and is included in
the catalogue given by G. Douglas, Virg. 476. 1.

———" Gan do double frangillis and gambettis,
" Danfis and roundis trafing mony gatis,
" Athir throw uthir reland on their gyfe,
" Thay futtit it fo, that lang war to devife
" Thare haifty fare, thare revelling and deray,
" Thare Morifis."

Junius explains it—Chironomica faltatio—faciem plerumq; in-
ficiunt fuligine, et peregrinum veftium cultum affumunt qui
ludicris talibus indulgent, ut *Mecuri* effe videantur ;—becaufe
this fpecies of dance was firft brought into Spain by the Moors,
and from the Spaniards it was communicated to other Euro-
pean nations, together with the *rebeck*, or *violin*, which is a
Moorifh inftrument.

Q STANZA

VI.

Then Steen cam ftappin in wi' ftends,
  Nae rynk might him arreft,
Splae-fut he bobbit up wi' bends,
  For Maufe he maid requeift;
                                    He

STANZA VI.

VER. 1. *Stends*] Long paces, or great fteps. G.
In old Scots, *to ftent*, to extend; a Lat. *tendere*. Douglas, p. 39. 34.

"Cruell Achil here *ftentit* his palzoun."

Ital. *ftendere*. Hence *ftend*. Douglas, defcribing horfes running off with the car, p. 338. 31.

"And brake away with the carte to the fchore,
"With *ftendis* fell."——

And p. 420. 53.

"Quhilk fleis forth fae wyth mony ane *ftend*."

VER. 2. *Rynk*] Sax. *rinc*. Homo robuftus, fortis, præftans, G. And hence it came to fignify, *a man* in general; as *wærcæft rinc*, fidus homo. *Rinc*, alfo ufed for hufband. Vide Cædmon. 4. 22. Lye, Sax. Lex. in *Rinc*. Here it means a ftrong man, or foldier, as it is alfo explained by Lye, Gloff. Sax. in Voce.

VER. 3. *Bobit up*] Jumped, or danced, with many bendings of the body. We find a fet of men, in the middle ages,
                                                              who

He lap quhyle he lay on his lends,
  But ryſand was ſae preiſt,
Quhyle he did hoaſt at baith the ends,
  For honour o' the feiſt,
    And dauns'd that day.

VII.

who, from the imperfect accounts given of them, appear to have been a kind of itinerant dancers, and, like their other wandering brethren, of no very good character. Urſtis. ap. Spelman. in *bobones, bubones,* lixæ, calones—Aliqando nebulones et Furciferi. Ger. *buben.* Chron. Colmar. ap. Cang. in *Bubii.* Servorum autem pauperum (in exercitu) qui dicuntur *bubii,* tanta fuit multitudo de *bobinare.* Conviciare, clamare, ap. Feſt. ubi vide Scaliger.

Bab, bow often, or ſink low, apud Anglos occidentales, to *bob,* or *bob* down. Gib.

VER. 5. *Lap*] Supped; lapt. A Cimbr. *lepia.* in Imperf. *lapte,* linqua vel lambendo bibere. G.

Surely our learned prelate has not attended to the obvious ſenſe of the paſſage: Our Poet deſcribes a clown dancing and leaping with ſuch violence as to fall. To *loup* is to *leap*; he *lap,* he leaped. Thus the Biſhop of Dunkeld, p. 418. 47.

—" Some in haiſt, with an *loupe* or ane ſwak,
" Thamſelf upcaſtis on the horſis bak."

Iſland. *ad hleypa,* to run; Sax. *hleapere,* ſaltator. Confer Jun. Gloſſ. in *Leap.*

Lends] Loins. Sax. *lendenu, lendena, lendene;* Iſl. *lendes,* Gib. From Iſl. *leinge,* to extend, this being the length of the trunk of the body.

VII.

Then Robene Roy begouth to revell,
And Towfie to him drugged.
Let be, quo' Jock, and caw'd him Jevel,
And be the tail him tuggit:
                                    Then

VER. 7. *Hoftit*] Anglis Sept. to *hoft*, eft tuffire. Sax. *hwofta*, eft tuffis; Ifl. *hooft*; Angl. occident. to huft, *i. e.* to cough violently. Gib.
Hoaft, *hoft*, cough; A. S. *hwofta*, from the Ifl. *boofte*, tuffis; Angl. Bor. *baufte*, id. a dry cough, as Ray explains it. Belg. *hoeft n* to cough.

STANZA VII.

VER. 1. *Revell*] To grow noify or troublefome. Belg, *ravelen, raveelen,* æftuare, circumcurfare. Skinner's etymology from Fr. *reveiller,* is ridiculous. We may here obferve, that of old the word *revel* did not fignify, as now, riot and diforder, but decent mirth and cheerfulnefs. So G. Douglas, p. 146. 48.
" With *revele,* blythnefs, and ane manere fere,
" Troyanis refavis thaim."

Chaucer alfo ufes it in the fame good fenfe; as alfo *riot*, in which he is followed too by the Bifhop, p. 37.
" The gild and *riot* Tyrrianis doublit for joy."
And p. 269. 46.
" The blisfull feift they making man and boy,
" So that thre hundredth rial temples ring,
" Of *riot*, rippet, and of *revelling*"

So

CHRIST's KIRK ON THE GREEN. 125

So the old French *rioter*, to feaft and be innocently merry. In this, however, they have departed from the original meaning of the Goth. *reta;* Ifland. *reita,* ad iram concitare. *Rede, raide,* anger. Inde Scot. *rede ;* Angl. *rate,* et præpofito, *wrath ;* Alam. *ratan,* irritare. It is more than probable that the ancient Latins ufed *ritare* in the fame fenfe ; and hence the etymon of *irritare* and *proritare,* which the modern etymologifts can make nothing of. From *riot,* the Barb. Lat. has formed *riota,* ufed in its original or bad fignification. So Statuta Colleg. Corifop. apud Cange, in *Riotta :* Ab omnibus contentionibus, rixis, jurgiis, convitiis, *riotis.* And ibid. Ad invicem tunc inceperunt magnam *riottam,* et fugerunt hinc inde. Ital. *riotta.* Villani Hift. l. 9. cap. 304. Venendo tra loro, a *riotta.* Fr. *riote.* So Hift. de la Guerre Sacr. ap. Cange. Par cette mariage fut faite concorde du Roi de France, et de celui de Caftele, de *riote* que eftoit entre eux. And the Poet, (ibid.)

" A tant commencent environ,
" A *rihotter* tout li Baron."

We have in King Rob. Brece's Life, *To riot all the land, i. e.* To plunder it.

VER. 2. *Drugged*] Came to him. Eft phrafis Cimbrica. *At draga till,* eft venire ad, vel in. Deut. 1. v. 2. *Draga yfer,* tranfire. V. 24. *Draga* ut, egredi. Deut. 3. 1. *Draga fram,* præcedere. V. 18. Gib.

We have little to add to the learned Bifhop's obfervation, but to remark the analogy of the languages derived from the Gothic. Thus A. G. *dragan;* Angl. *draw.* In the ancient laws of Wefter Gothland, ap. Ihre, Lex. in *Draga,* it is written *Draha, Ar eig or hufum drahit,* fi ex ædibus portatum non fuit, in the fame fenfe as the Latin *traho,* Fr. *trainer. Draga wagnen,* to draw a waggon. Afthmatic people are faid *draga andam* in the fame fenfe almoft as the

Latins,

Latins, spiritum *trahere*. Vide Liv. l. 4. cap. 21. *Draga not*, to draw a net. Whence our small net, thrown with the hand, is called a *drag-net*. We may also hence derive the name of that species of net, called by the Latins *tragulæ*, a *trahendo*, says Turneb. Adverf. l. 20. c. 14. Vide Plin. l. 16. c. 8. Isidorus calls it *tragum*. Metaphorically *Draga sin wæg*, to go away. Lat. *viam ducere;* Belg. *trecken*. Adde Cange in *Traho*, where he notes the origin of the French *tirer vers un lieu*. It is used also to signify *doubting*, the mind being drawn hither and thither. *Han nager vid sig*, deliberat de hac re. We find quite a similar phrase, Sallust. Bell. Jugurth. cap. 93. Marius multis diebus et laboribus consumptis, anxius *trahere* cum animo suo, omitteret ne inceptum, an fortunam opireretur. *Te deceive.* Laur. Petri de missa, ap. Ihre, ubi sup. *Christen almoga hafwær latit talje och dragha sig*. Populus Christianus se decipi passus est. Franc. *trahir*, to deceive or betray.

VER. 3. *Jevel*] Vox blandientis, forsan idem quod jewel. Gib.

We cannot agree with the Bishop in this interpretation. These people are about to quarrel, and therefore *jevel* must here be a term of reproach ; perhaps an evil-spirit or dæmon. Goth. *jette*, giant; Island. *gotun*. The Saxons call a giant *Eten ;* and hence, perhaps, the Scots *Redeten*, the name of a Giant or Dæmon used by nurses to frighten their children. *Jettegrytor*, ollæ gigantum, round holes in the rocks, in which (say the vulgar) the Giants or Dæmons cooked their victuals. Uncertain as we are of the true reading of the MS. we only hazard this as mere conjecture.

VER. 4. *Tuggit*] Drew. Scots *tugge*, to draw, from the Goth. *tahjan*, lacerare, discerpere. Ulph. Mark ix. 26. *Filu tahjands ina*, Greatly fearing him. Adde Luke ix. 42. Hence, as the learned Ihre observes, (in voce) *tugga*, to eat,

The Kenzie clieked to a kevel,
God wots if thir twa luggit;
They parted manly wi' a nevel,
Men fay that hair was ruggit
 Betwixt them twa.
VIII.

eat, to *tear* with the teeth, as in chewing. Ifl. *toga;* A. S. *teogan,* trahere. Confer Ihre, Lex. 2. p. 973.

VER. 5. *Kenzie*] The angry man. A. S. *Kene, ken wer,* Vir acer, iracundus.

Clieked] Catched up, or fnatched. Gib.
Click, in old Englifh, apprehendere, rapere. Ifland. *kla,* frico. *Ad klaa,* fricare. Hence *claw,* and *to claw.* Sax. *clawan,* fcabere. Perhaps *klick* is only a contraction of the Saxon *gelæccan,* apprehendere.

.' *Kevel, or Gevel*] So it fhould be wrote, and not erroneoufly, as in Ramfay's edition, *cavell.* It is properly a long pole, ftaff, or fpear. Goth. *gafflack,* jaculi genus, apud Vet. Suio-Gothos, fays the ingenious Ihre, in voce. Snorro, tom. 1. p. 367. *Olafr K. fcaut ftundum bogafcoti, enn ftundumga flocum,* King Olaf fometimes fought with the bow, and fometimes ufed the dart. A. S. *gafelucas.* Matthew Paris, ad an. 1256. p. 793. Frifones—ipfum Williefmum cum jaculis, quæ vulgariter *gaveloces* appellant—e veftigio hoftiliter infequebantur. Hence the French *javelle, javelot,* and our *javelin. Gaffel,* Ihre explains, *Quicquid bifurcum eft,* as a hay-fork. Hence Scot. *gavelok,* an iron crow, or lever, as it is generally divided into two toes at the lower end. Pelletier, Dict. Celt. derives it from two Celtic words, *galf,* bifidus,

VIII.

Ane bent a bow, sic sturt could steir him,
Grit skayth wead to haif skard him:
He cheist a flane as did effeir him;
   The toder said, Dirdum, Dardum.

                                  Through

bifidus, and *flach*, scipio, ut adeo denotet baculum bifurcum. Welsh *gefa*, il, forceps.

VER. 6. *Luggit*] Pulled each other about. Goth. *lugga*, crines vellere; A. S. *geluggian*, vellere; Isl. *lagd*, villum notat; *lugg*, villus, sign. any cloth or other thing which has been made rough by carding. Hence, perhaps, the Greek λαγος, hirsutus; and the name of the hare in that language, λαγωπος, alias δασυπυς.

It is not easy to give a reason for Bishop Gibson deriving this Scots word from Cimbr. *liuga*, fingere; Sax. *leogan*; Goth. *linga*, mendacium. Nothing can be more foreign to the obvious meaning of the passage. In old English, *lug* signifies to draw or pull.

VER. 7. *Nevel*] Alapa, (says Gibson, Not. in Polem. Middin.) a blow or box on the ear, qua quis prosterni potest. Verb *nevel*, to box. Cimbr. *hneffe*, pugnus. Scotis *neaf*, (rectius *nief*, or *nieve*) et *fella*, prosternere. Angl. *to fell*. Dougl. Virg. 123. 45.

    " And smytand with *nieffis* her briest."

Bruce's Life, p. 431.

    " And als their *nives* aft samen drive."

                                       STANZA

STANZA VIII.

VER. 1. *Sturt*] Wrath, anger, defpite. *Sturt* is ufed actively by Chaucer, to ftrive or contend. A. S. Alem. Cimbr. *ſtrid*, and *ſtrit*. Gloſſ. apud Jun. in *Striſe*, altercatio. *Strit*, feditio. *Heim ſtrit*, dimicant, pugnant, ftrident. Iſland. *ſtryd*; Germ. *ſtreiten*, to fight; Iſl. *ſtir*, bellum. In Suio-Goth. *Storto*, præcipitem agere, deturbare. *Storta en i olycka*; aliquem in infortunium præcipitem dare. Germ. *ſturtzen*, *genſtortig*, contumax; *paſtorta*, irruere. Iſl. *ſtyr*, conflictus. Hence the old French *eſtour*, and our *ſtour*, heat of battle, often ufed by the old poets: Douglas, 387. 4.

" The *ſloure* encreſſis, furius and wod."

Life of Bruce, p. 293.

" The *ſloure* begouth."

He alfo ufes the word *ſturt* to fignify *vexation*, 41. 36.

" Dolorus my lyfe I led in *ſturt* and pane."

And p. 238. 21.

" *Sturtin* ſtudy has the ſtere."——

Confer Rudd. Gloſſ. ibid. in *Sturt*.

VER. 2. *Skaith*] Damage, hurt, lofs. In our old laws, *ſkaithleſs to keep*, to preferve from harm. Douglas, 72 23.

——" How grete harme and ſkaith, for evermair,

" That child has caught."——

And. p. 41. v. 43.

" To me this was firſt appearance of ſkaithe."

A. S. *ſkeathian*, *ſcaethan*; Teuton. *ſchaden*, to hurt. Vide Lye, Sax. Dict. Theot. *Skadon*, damnum, noxa; et Goth. *Skathjan*, nocere. A. S. *ſceathe*; Teuton. *ſchade*.

Skar'd] To have affrighted or hindered him, Douglas, 214. 52.

R.

Through baith the chieks he thoch to chier him,
Or through the erſs haif chard him;
Be ane akerbraid it came na' neir him,
I canna' tell quhat mard him,
Sae wide that day.

IX.

" Ne *ſkar* not at his freyndis face, as ane gaiſt."
Uſed alſo actively, to *ſcare*, to *terrify* ; *ſcare-crow*, a figure uſed to fright away birds. Heſych. interprets σκαριζ:]αι, ταρατ]ι]αι, turbatur; and Euſtath. σκαριζειν, palpitare.

VER. 3. *Cheiſt*] Or cheſid, *i. e.* chooſed. Thus Douglas too uſes it. Alam. *kieſen*, eligere, from the Iſland. *kiooſa*, eligere.

Flane] Arrow, alſo written *flaine*. Angl. S. *flan*, *flæn*. Perhaps (ſays Lye) from *fleogan* or *fleon*, volare. Iſland. *flein*, an arrow. Douglas, 387.

———" Fleand with her bow ſchute mony ane flane."

Effeir] For this is the true reading; not as in Ramſay, *affeir*. He choſe out ſuch an arrow as ſuited his hand. This is an ordinary term in old our laws : *As effeirs*, as belongs to, as is proper and expedient. *Efferand*, or *effering*, conform to, proper to. Vide Ruddim. Gloſſ. ad G. Douglas.

Efferis alſo ſignifies buſineſs. Douglas, p. 359. 48.
" The greateſt part of our werkis and *efferis*
" Ben endit now."———
Unleſs this be only another mode of ſpelling *affairs*.

VER. 4. *Dirdum dardum*] Term of deriſion; a great ado about nothing. Seems to be formed from the Iſland *dyr*, pretioſus ; or rather from *dyrd*, gloria, *dyrka*, glorifico. The

other

IX.

Wi' that a frien o' his cried, Fy!
And up an arrow drew;
He forgit it fae forcefully,
The bow in flinders flew.

Sic
other word seems to be added only, *euphoniæ gratiæ*, unless
it be also from the Island. *daare,* rash; whence our verb, to
dare.

VER. 6. *Chard*] This is another part of the verb *cheir*, in
the verse before. Perhaps it may come from Goth. *karfwa*,
minutim cædere. Sax. *ceorfan, beceorfan,* amputare; *ceorf-æx,*
securis. Hence *char* signifies to *wound,* or *cut*; and our
carve, to divide or cut meat into small pieces.

VER. 8. *Mard*] Spoilt his shooting; made him err so
wide. Sax. *amyrran,* distrahere, consumere; Aleman.
merren, to hinder; Isl. *meru,* minutim, dissipare; *marde,*
dissipavi.

STANZA IX.

VER. 3. *Forgit*] Pressed. Isl. *fergia.* In Præter. *Fergde,*
premere, compingere. G.
Farg, Pressura, apud Verelium. Hence, perhaps, our
word *fardel,* burden. " *Ferg,*" (says Ihre) " vocantur conti,
" qui ad continendum corticem, quo domus ruricolarum te-
" guntur, fastigio utrinq; dimittuntur." From this idea of
pressing,

Sik was the will of God, trow I ;
For, had the tree been trew,
Men said, that ken'd his archery,
He wald haif slain enow,
　　　　　Belyve that day.

X.

preſſing, perhaps the name of a ſmith's *forge* is derived ; at leaſt, this etymology may be as juſt as thoſe mentioned by Menage and Junius, in *Forge*. Biſhop Douglas calls a ſmith *forgeare*, and a forge *forgin*.

VER. 4. *Flinders*] Splinters. Biſhop Douglas writes it *flendris*, and Mr Ruddiman (in Gloſſ. ad Virg.) deduces it from Lat. *findere*, Fr. *fendre*. But the true origin is the Gothic *flinga ;* fruſtum, utpote quod percutiendo rumpitur, ſays the learned Ihre. *Isflinger*, pieces of broken ice. And theſe from *flenga*, tundere, percutere ; Gr. φλαω, ferio. Hence, too, Germ. *flegel*, our *flail*, and the Fr. *fleau*. From this idea, the Icelanders call a wedge *fleigr*, and the Suio-Goths *plugg*, in the ſame ſenſe as we uſe it, *viz*. a piece of wood driven into a hole. Vide Ihre, Lex. in *Plugg*. This moſt accurate etymologiſt thinks that the ancient Iſlanders pronounced *flæc*, ſegmentum, fruſtum, partem de toto demptam. If this origin be juſt, we have here the real meaning of the A. S. *flicce*, and our *flitch*, as expreſſing a part of the carcaſe of the ſow. Iſland. *flycke*. In Trygwaſ. Saga, p. ii. p. 23. *Fleickis ſneid*, fruſtum lardi. Confer Ihre, Lex. in v. *Flaca*, findere, partiri. Jun. in *Flitch*.

VER. 7. *That kend*] Scribe *quha* kend.

Kend

Kend, From *kunna*, Goth. *scire*. Ulphila, *kunnan*, to know. Joh. vii. 27. *Kunnum*. Adde John xiv. ver. 4. Hesychius has κοννιιτ, scire ; *kunnist*, scientia, now pronounced *konst*; *kunnoga*, notum facere ; *kunnog*, sciens, peritus. Knytl. Saga, p. 4. " *Harald K. baud cunnugum* " *mannum*;" " King Harald consulted the Diviners ;" or, as we say, the *cunning men*. Hence, he who attends to the course of the ship is said to *cunn* the ship. Transferred also to denote bodily strength, if this be not its primary signification. Al. *chunnan*, posse, valere, Germ. *chonnen*. Anglice *can*.

VER. 8. *Enow*] Enough, many. Sax. *genog*, *genoh*, satis; Goth. *ganohs*, multus ; Isl. *gnoght*, *nogt*, abundance ; *gnogr* vel *nogr*, abundantia. G.

In Ulphila, Joh. xiv. 8. *Gana unsis*, sufficit nobis. Alam. *genuoh*, any, enough.

VER. 9. *Belyve*] Sensus hujus vocis constat ex Versione G. Douglas, ubi sic redditur hoc carmen.

" *Extemplo Æneæ solvuntur frigore membra.*"

" *Belive* Æneas' members schuke for cauld ;" Et istud,

" *Ut primum lux alma data est.*"

" *Belive* as that the halesum day wox licht."

Quibus adde:

" How Æneas in Afric did arrive,
" And that with schote slew seaven hartis *belive*." G.

Mr Ruddiman would derive this word from Teuton. *blick*, nictus oculi. We in Scotland say, A thing was done in a *blink*, suddenly ; from Isl. *blinka* nictare ; *ogonblick*, nictus oculi. In the ancient Ballad of *William of Cloudeslie*, (Rel. of Anc. Poetry, vol. 1. p. 164.)

" The

X.

An hasty hensure, callit Hary,
Quha was an archer heynd,
Tytt up a taikel withoutten tary,
That torment sae him teynd.

"The fyrst boone that I wold aske,
"Ye wold graunt it me *belyse.*"
Ibid. p. 91.

"He thoght to loose him *belive.*"

STANZA X.

Bishop Gibson places here the Stanza beginning,
"A zape young man that stood him neist," &c.
which is the XII. in Ramsay's edition.

VER. 1. *Hensure*] So Ramsay. Gibson has here *kinsman*; we know not on what authority. *Hein, heini,* Celt. strong young man. V. Bullet in *Heini.* It would seem that the copy followed by the Bishop was very faulty; or perhaps he left out this word, because he did not understand it.

VER. 2. *Heynd*] Lord H. in his Gloss. to the Ancient Scots Poems, explains it *handy, expert.* Douglas, p 363. 53.

———"Eneas *heynd,* curtas, and gude."
And p. 306. v. 3.

———"Clitius the *heynd.*"

Skinner writes *hende,* which he explains, *feat, fine, gentle.*

VER.

I wat na' quhidder his hand cou'd vary,
Or the man was his frien';
For he efcapit, throw the michts of Mary,
As man that nae ill meind,
But gude that day.

XI.

VER. 3. *Tytt up a taikle*] Made ready an arrow. Chaucer:

"Well could he drefs his *tackle* yomenly."

And:

"The *tackle* fmote, and depe it went." G.

Douglas ufes the fame often: Thus, p. 300. v. 1.

"His bow with hors fenonnis bendit has he,
"Tharin ane *tackill* fet of fouir tree."

And below, (ibid.)

"Quhirrand fmertly furth flaw the *takyll* tyte."

Tackle, Goth. fig. ornamenta navis, rudentes. Ihre, in Lex. *Tackle*; and hence we fay the *tacklss*, the ropes of a fhip.

VER. 4. *That torment fae him teyñd*] So Ramfay. The Bifhop reads:

"I trow the man was tien."

Not having the MSS. we cannot judge which is the true reading. *Torment* is ufed by our old writers to fignify *wrath, anger, indignation*.

VER. 4. *Teyñd*] *Tien*, incenfed; Sax. *teona*, irritatio. G.

Teen,

Teen, and, as Chaucer writes it *tene*, injury, vexation. Sax. *teonan*, injuriæ, calumniæ; Belg. *tenenn, tanen*, irritare. τειvεϑαι, vexare. Vide Junius, in *Teen*.

VER. 5. *I wat na'*] I know not. Goth. *wetan*, fcire. Ulph. *vitan*; Ifland. *vita*; Germ. *wiſſen*. The Latin, with the digamma, hence forms *video*. The A. S. for *vitan*, put often *wiſtan*. Hence our *wiſt*; *I Wiſt not*. Non multum abludit ειδω, ειδεω, quæ de acie tammentis quam oculorum ufurpantur; as the moſt ingenious critic Ihre obſerves, in *Weta*. The Goths diſtinguiſh betwixt *bokwett*, artium fcientia, and *manweett*, humanitas; and indeed they are often found feparate.

VER. 6. *Or the man was his frien'*] Biſhop Gibfon reads thus:

"Or his foe was his friend."

Which is fcarcely to be underſtood.

VER. 7. *Michts of Mary*] Through the protection of the Virgin. Every body knows, that the blind votaries of Popery more frequently addreſs themfelves in prayer to the Virgin Mary, than either to God or our Bleſſed Saviour. The Scots fay *mights*, power, from Ulphil. *mahts, magan*, poſſe. Mark xiv. v. 20. *Ni mag qwiman*. Non poſſum venire. Iſl. *At meiga*.

VER. 8. *As man*, &c.] Biſhop Gibfon has it:

"As one that nothing meant."

But I know not on what authority. He has either ufed unwarrantable liberties with the text, or has been miſled by fome erroneous copy.

STANZA

XI.

Then Lowry lyke a lyon lap,
An' fone a flane can fedder;
He hecht to perfe him at the pap,
Theron to wad a wedder.

He

STANZA XI.

VER. 1. *Lap*] Run, a Cimbr. *Hlaupa*, in Imp. *hliop* currere. Vel *leapt*, a Sax. *leapan*, faltare, currere. Imperf. *Laup*. G.
The laft etymology is the true one; from *laup* we fay, *to loup*, to jump. Thus Douglas, Virg. p. 418.

—— " Sume in haift, with ane *loupe* and ane fwak,
" Thamefelf upcaftis on the horfis bak."

Goth. *lopa*, currere. Hence *loppa*, a flea. Ulphila writes *hlaupan*, faltare. Mark, chap. x. ver. 5. *Uſhlaupands*, exilians. Jun. in Gloff. Ulphil. thinks this has fome connection with λαυρθαζει, which Hefychius explains ςπευδει, haftens.

VER. 2. *Flane*] Vide Note to Stanza VIII.

VER. 3. *Hecht*] Hoped. A. Sax. *hiht*, fpes. G.
Hecht, he promifed to himfelf, or vowed. So LL. Goth. cap. 4. 1. (ap. Ihre in *Heta)* Engin ma haita a huathki a hult epa hauga. Nemo vota nuncupabit, nec luco nec tumulo. Ulphila *gahaitan*. Vide Mark xiv. 11. Al. *heizan*. Gloff. Lipfii, *Giheitan*. Ifland. *heita*, unde *heit* votum. *Streinga heit*, voto fe obligare.

He hit him on the wame a wap,
It buft like ony bledder;
But fwa his fortune was and hap,
His doublet made o' lether
Saift him that day.

XII.

VER. 4. *Wad*] Pawn. Goth. *wad*, pignus; A. S. *wed*, *wedde fyllan*, pignus dare. Fenn. *weden*. We muft obferve here, for the illuftration of this phrafe, that *wad* properly fignifies *cloth*; becaufe, in the fcarcity of cafh of old, cloth was given as ready money, and received as fuch for other goods. Hence, when any pledge was given, it was generally *cloth*, wad; and from the frequency of this cuftom, *wad* came to fignify a *pledge*. We ftill fay, the *wadding* of a gun. By the common change of *f* and *w*, the Iflanders pronounce *fat*, and *fot*. Alam. *pfand*; Goth. *pant*, *pans*; Lat. *pignus*. Hence the Goth. verb *wadfætta*, oppignorare, and the Scots law-term *wadfett*, and *to wadfet*, to lay in pawn. In the middle Latin we find *vadium, guadium*, &c. Etrard in Græcifmo, ap. Cange in Vadium.

" Vado viam, vado quadrupedem, vadio, vadium do,
" Pro conforte vador; fonat hoc quod fum fidejuffor."

Hence *vadimoniare*. Vide plura ap. Cange in *Vadium*, et in *Plegius*. Alfo called *gagium*, unde Fr. *gage*; and from hence the *gage*, offered by the challenger, and taken up by the perfon challenged, in furety that he was to fight the other.

VER. 5. *Wap*] A blunt or edgelefs ftroke, in oppofition to one that pierces the fkin. The elegant Editor of the Scots Poems, printed Edinburgh, 1770, explains *wapped*, fuddenly ftruck down, that is, by a *blunt ftroke*, as of a cudgel.

VER.

CHRIST's KIRK ON THE GREEN. 139

VRR. 6. *Buft*] Sounded; a dull found, fuch as a bladder filled with wind makes, when ftruck. *Puff* of wind; flatus venti. Fr. *bouffeè* de vent; Belg. *boffen*, to puff up the cheeks with wind. Hence *buffet*, a blow on the cheek. Dan. *puff*, plaga, ictus. *Puffe*, percutere malas inflatas. Hence, too, vain-glorious boafters are called by the Dutch *poffen* and *poechan*. Gr. Ποιφυσσειν, vehementius fpirare. Fr. *piaffe*, pomp, vain glory.

VER. 8. *Doublet of lether*] Our anceftors wore very commonly clothes made of leather; and anciently the inhabitants of this ifland ufed no other garments. But even long after the ufe of woollens, thofe who lived much in the woods, and the yeomanry, were often clad in fkins. Thus Guy of Gifborn is dreffed, Rel. of Anc. Poet. vol. 1. p. 83.

" And he was clad in his capul hyde,
" Top, and tayle, and mayne."

We in this ifland had this cuftom from our German, and they from their Scythian anceftors, of whom Juftin, l. 2. c. 2. " Lanæ iis ufus, ac veftium ignotus, quanquam continuis fri-
" goribus urantur, pellibus tamen ferinis, aut murinis, utun-
" tur." Adde Ifidor. lib. 19. cap. 23. and Cæfar of the Suevi, lib. 4. cap. 1. Cluver. Geogr. l. 1. c. 16. We find the Emperor Charlemagn clothed with a fkin above his inner garments. Eginhart, Tit. Car. cap. 23. defcribing his drefs, " Veftitu patrio, hoc eft Francico utebatur,—crura et pedes
" calceamentis conftringebat, et ex pellibus Lutrinis, thorace
" confecta, humeros ac pectus hieme muniebat." This garment was by the ancient Iflanders called *felldr*, being made of fheep-fkin with the wool on, and ferved them as a cover for their beds at night, as well as a cloke, or robe, through the day. Thus Ara Frode, Libell. de Ifland. cap 7. defcribing Thorgeir going to bed, " Oc bræiddi felld fin a fic, et explicabat
" ftragulum

XII.

The buff fae boift'roufly abaift him,
That he to th' erd dufht down;
The ither man for deid there left him,
An' fled out o' the town.

The

" ftragulum fuum fuper fe." It is ftill cuftomary in Greenland, Iceland, Finland, and Lapland, to fleep on fkins, and alfo in Norway. Vid. Buff. Lex. ad ara Frode in *Felldr*, Even the women of diftinction wore their *feld* in the day time. So the Norwegian poet of Gudruna:

" Som det nu lakked till quelden
" Indkom Fru Guru med *felden*."

" In the evening came in the Lady Gudruna clothed in her " *feld*."

STANZA XII.

We give this Stanza from Gibfon's edition. It is not in Ramfay's, though by the ftile it appears to be genuine.

VER. 1. *Buff*] Vide Supra, Stanza 11. *Buff*, fays Gibfon, a blow or ftroke.

Abaift] Abafed, aftonifhed, fays Gibfon.

Perhaps it fhould be *abafhed;* confternatus, ftupefactus. Suid. Αβαζος, ησυχος, ηγεν εςρημενος τε βαζειν, ὁ εςι λεγειν; filens, cui ereptus eft ufus loquendi. Chaucer has *abawed* for abafhed. I was *abawed* for merveile.

Jun.

The wives came forth, an' up thay reft him,
An' fand lyfe in the lown;
Then wi' three routs on's erfe they reir'd him,
An' cur'd him out o' foone,
Frae hand that day.

XIII.

Jun. derives it from Sax. *beap;* de quo vide Lye, Sax. Dict. Confer Jun. in *Bafe.*

VER. 2. *Dufht*] Fell down fuddenly. *Dufch,* contundere, allidere. Douglas, p. 225. 1.

" The fharp hedit fchaft *dufchit* with the dint."

And p. 296. 34.

" The birnand towris down rollis with ane ruche,
" Quhil all the hevynnefs dynlit with the *dufche.*"

VER. 5. *Wives*] Women. *Wif,* ap. Sax. et *twif,* ap. Cimbr. fæminam, vel mulierem fignificat. Gib.

Thus, Gen. iii. 2. xx. 5. *This wyf;* This woman. Adde Cædmon, 58. 9. Matth. ix. 20. *An wyf,* quædam mulier. Jo. iv. 9. *Samaritanifce wyf,* A Samaritan woman. Gen. v. 2. *Were and wif,* Man and woman, male and female. Vide plura ap. Lye, in *Wif.* Hence *wiman, wimman,* i. e. *wif—man,* Mulier, fæmina. Alam. *Uuib, Uuip;* Germ. *weif.* The learned Ihre mentions two derivations; firft, a *wefwa,* to weave; or elfe from *wif,* or *hwif,* calantica, a woman's head-drefs, metaphorically, as the northern writers fay, Gyrdle oc linda, *Girdel and belt,* for man and woman; and alfo *hatt oc hætta,* pileus et vitta, in the fame fenfe.

VER. 5. *Reft him*] Snatched. Sax. *reafian,* rapere. G. Hence

Hence Douglas uses it for robbed, pulled, or forced away, 74. 12.

"The rayne and roik *reft* from us ficht of hevin."

Teut. *rauben*, spoliare; *raffen*, corripere. Hence *bereave, bereft*; and the Scots, *to reave*; and *reaver*, a robber, often used for a *pirate*. Hist. of Wallace, p. 342.

"Upon the sea yon *reaver* long has been."

And p. 343.

"At ilka shot he gart a *reaver* die."

Reif, rapine, robbery. G. Douglas, p. 354. 30.

"For na conquest, *reif*, stayt, nor pensioun."

Ver. 6. *Loun*] Rogue, rascal. Alludit. Eng. *clown*. Douglas, p. 239.

——"Quod I, *Loun*, thou leis."

The old ballad of Gilderoy, Reliq. Anc. Poet. p. 324.

"And bauldly bare away the gear
"Of many a lawland *loun*."

Lye Addit. to Junius deduces it from Cimbr. *luin*; ignavus, piger, iners.

Ver. 7. *Routs*] Roarings, bellowings. Cimb. *at ryta*, vel *rauta*; frendere, vel rugire belluarum more. Angli Bor. dicunt, The ox *rowts*; et hinc ap. Scotos *route*, est idem as to make a great noise. Ut habet Douglas:

"The firmament gan rummil, rare, and *rout*."

Hinc, oborto tumultu dicimus, What a *rout* is here? Item *orto strepitu*, What a *rout* you make? G. Dougl.

"The are begouth to rumbill and *rout*."

Sax. *hrutan*, to snort, to snore in sleeping. This is Mr Ruddiman's etymon; but we imagine it comes more immediately
from

XIII.

A zape zung man that ftude him neift,
Lous'd aff a fchot wi' yre;
He ettlit the bern in at the brieft,
The bolt flew owre the byre.

Ane

from the Goth. *hropian*, clamare. Ulphila, Matth. xxvii. 46. *Ufropida ftibnai mikilai*, clamavit voce magna. Luke xix. 40. *Hropjand*, clamabunt. Ifland. *hroop*, clamor; Alam. *ruafan*, clamare, vociferare. Is *roopy*, hoarfe, derived from this?

VER. 8. *Frae hand*] Quickly, in a little time. Ang. out of hand. G.

STANZA XIII.

This is the 12th in Ramfay's edition, owing to the omiffion of the foregoing, which we give from the Bifhop's edition; but this 13th Stanza is omitted by Gibfon.

VER. 1. *Zaip*, or *Zape*] Ready, alert. We have already faid why our old writers always ufe the *z* for the *y* Englifh, when it begins the word, as *zeir*, *yeir*—*zour*, *your*, &c. Douglas, p. 409. v. 19.

" The biffy knapis and verlotis of his ftabil,
" About thyme ftude, full *zape* and ferviabil."

It may alfo mean vaunting, infulting. Chaucer thus ufes it. R. R. 1927.

" And

" And fayd to me in great *jape*,
" Yeld the, for thou may not efcape."

Ifland. *geip*, boafting. Chaucer, Lucre. v. 18.

——" Tarqinius the yonge
" Gan far to *jape*, for he was light of tonge."

Hence it came to fignify jefting, light talking. Id. Fr. lib. 2. 1167.

" He gan his beft *japes* forth to caft,
" And made her fo to laugh."——

Neift] Next. In Decalog. Angl. Sax. Ne wilna thu, thines *nehftan* yrfes med unriht ; Ne concupifcas bona proximi tui injufte. *Neh*, nigh; *nehft*, neareft. Hence *neh-bur*, neighbour, from Ulphila's *neguha*, nigh. Mark ii. 4. *Neguha gwiman*, To come near. Alem. *nah*; Bel. *nae*, *naer*. Whence our Scots *naar*, near.

VER. 3. *Ettlit*] Defigned, aimed, intended. Cimbr. *Atætla*, defignare, deftinare.

" The goddes *ettilit*, if werdes were not contrare." G.

Ætla (fays the learned Ihre) indicat varios mentis humanæ motus, ut dum deftinatæ fibi proponit, judicat, fperat, &c. Ifland. id. Thorften Wik, S. p. 10. *Dat ætla eg*. Id Spero, vel animo concipio. Lex. Scanica, p. 16. fect. 21. *Ætla wider frænda fin;* Confultare cum cognatis, vel amicis fuis. Confonat Gr. εθελω, nec fenfu longius diftat, quum utrumq; defiderium voluntatis ad quidpiam tendens denotat.

Barn] The A. Sax. *bearn*; Ifl. *barn*; a *bairan*, *beran*, parere. Gib.

It is is originally derived from the Goth. *barns*. Vide Ulphila, Luke i. 41. and ii. 12. We find it even ufed to fignify a girl, Mark v. 39, 40. Hence *barnilo*, a little boy, an infant. Luke i. 46. *Jah thu barnilo*, And thou child. Alam.
barn,

barn, bern. Let us obferve, by the way, that our old authors often ufe *bairn,* to denote young men, full-grown perfons, as the Englifh do *child.* So Pallas, addreffing Æneas, ap. Douglas, p. 244. 33.

" Come furth, quhatever thou be, *berne* bald."

And p. 439. 22.

―――" And that awfull *berne,*
" Beryng fchaftis fedderit."―――

Bern time, the whole number of a woman's children. Id. p. 443.

" Bare at ane birth―――
" The nicht thare moder, that *barne time* miferabill."

The ancient Englifh writers apply *child* to knights. Thus the Child of Elle, Reliq. of Anc. Poetry, p. 107.

" And yonder lives the *Child* of Elle,
" A young and comely knight."

Warburton, Not. on Shakefpeare, obferves, that in the times of chivalry, the noble *youth,* who were candidates for knighthood, during the time of their probation, were called *Infans, Varlets, Damoyfels, Bacheliers.* From this comes the Scots word *chiel,* which is applied to a young man, full-grown.

VER. 4. *Bolt*] Arrow. Sagitta capitata, fays Junius. Cymbr. *Bollt.* Belg. *bolt, bout.* Non abludit βελις, jaculum; βολιδες, miffilia; a βαλλω, jacio.

Byre] Cowhoufe. Theotif. *Buer* eft cafa, tugurium. Item. *byre* eft villa, fiquidem *bœr* eft pagus, villa prædium. Gib.

In the old Gothic *byr,* pagus; a *bo,* habitare. Alfo *by,* pagus. Hefych. βυριο, οικημα, habitatio. Etym. Mag. ευβυριον pro ευοικον, and βυριοθεν, Hefych. pro οικοθεν. " Qumque aliæ olim urbes non fuerint, quam grandi- " ores

Ane cryd, Fy! he had flain a prieft,
 A myle bezond a myre;
Then bow and bag frae him he keift,
 And fled as ferfs as fire
  Frae flint that day.

XIV.

" ores villæ, hinc etiam urbes quantumvis ampliores, idem
" nominis habuere, et etiamnum inter Danos habent,"
fays the learned Ihre. Hence. *By fogde,* Præfectus civitatis.
By lag, Jus civitatis, who fornandes de reb. Get. tranflates
bellago, *byfwen,* city-officer, or conftable. *Byr,* an inhabitant;
A. S. *bure;* Germ. *bauer.*

VER. 5. *Slain a prieft*]. This was, in thofe days of ignorance, deemed the moft horrid murder that could be committed, and in a manner irremiffible, the perfon of a prieft being held much more facred than that of any layman. Hence, in the laws of the middle ages, we find the fine, or compenfation for the murder of a prieft, much higher than that of a layman, of whatever high rank he might be. They were eftimated according to their feveral degrees; and hence, in the laws of Kanute, p. 151. we find Tryhyndmon, Syxhyndmon, *i. e.* Homo ducentorum, trecentorum, fexcentorum folidorum; every man's life, from the king to that of the cottager, having a fixed price fet upon it. This was generally called *wiregild, wergild,* and *manwyrd, the price of a man.* By the laws of King Athelftan, the King's life is valued at 30,000 thrymfas; an Archbifhop's at one half of this fum. A common man's life is bought for 267 thrymfas; but a bifhop's at 8000; and one in fimple prieft's orders at 2000. In the additions to the Salic law, made by the Emperor Louis, anno 819, we find

the

XIV.

Wi' forks and flails they lent grit flaps,
 And flang togidder like fryggs;
Wi' bougars of barns thay beft blew kapps,
 Quhyle thay of berns maid briggs.

The

the compenfation for a prieſt always triple to that of a layman; and if the offender had not wherewith to pay, he was fold for a flave.

Ver. 7. *Bag*] The quiver of arrows, which was often made of the ſkin of a beaſt.

Kieſt] Caſt.

STANZA XIV.

Ver. 1. *Flaps*] Douglas writes it *flappis*, ſtrokes given with a blunt weapon, ſuch as a flail. Hence Belg. *flabbe*, colaphus, a ſono, ſays Ruddiman. *Flap*, ſays Jun. extremitas cujufq; rei mollis ac pendula, quæq; ad levem motum ſtatim concutitur. Ita *throat-flap*, Anglis eſt epiglottis. *Flye-flap*, muſcarium. Teuton. *flabbe*, libens; præfixo D. Hence, too, Suio-Goth. *flab*, us, labium, de quo vid. Ihre, Lex. in *Flabb*, who, with his uſual accuracy, obſerves the connection betwixt the Greek and Scythian languages; riſum nempe, qui patulo ore, et diductis labiis fit, perinde in illa (Lingua Græca) πλατυν γελωτα dici, ac a nobis *flatt loje*. We

ſay

say alſo, a *broad* laugh, a *broad* ſtare. Perhaps *flatter* may be alſo derived fro *flat*, de quo vide Jun. in *Flatter*.

VER. 2. *Fryggs*] Perhaps this is the ſame as *freik*, ap. Douglas, a fooliſh impertinent fellow. Teuton. *frech*, protervus, procax. Petulans, ſays Mr Ruddiman; unde Angl. *freik*, whim or caprice. In the Jus Aulicum of King Magnus, anno 1319. ſect. 9. we find ſome public game or meeting, called *frimark*, prohibited on account of the miſchiefs and wrongs they did to each on theſe occaſions. Framledis forbjudher minne herre nokor frimark, &c. ulterius prohibita eſſe vult dominus meus omnia ludicra, *frimark* dicta, ſive equo peragantur, ſive alias. Confer Ihre in *Frimark*. Theſe ſports were alſo called *ſeylemarked*, de quo id. ibid. Vide Jus Aulicum, Dan. anno 1590. ſect. 25.

Friggs] Forſan eagerly, libenter, a Cimb. *frigd*, libido. Gibſ. vide infra, Stanza 21. v. 4. Note.

VER. 3. *Bougars*] Rafters; probably from A. S. *bugan flectere*, unde *boh*, boga, a bough or branch.

VER. 4. *Beſt*] Beat. Thus the word is uſed by G. Douglas.

Blew kapps] Alluding to the blue caps or bonnets our commonalty uſually wear on their heads.

VER. 4. *Briggs*] Bridges. The elegant etymologiſt Ihre obſerves, that the original word is *bro*, ſignifying *ſtratum aliquod*—Nunc obſervare lubet (adds he) ſeptentrionem noſtrum ſolum eſſe, qui hoc primitivum retinuerit, dum cæteri dialecti omnes diminutivum ejus adoptarunt. Such is *brigga*, from *bro*; *bygga*, from *bo*; *ſugga*, from *ſo*, &c. Hence, too, the Suio-Goth. *broſſol*, tabulatum pontis; *brokiſta*, fulcimentum pontis; *bookar*, idem; *brygga*, a bridge; A. S. *brigg*, *brycge*; Germ. *brucke*. Obſerve here, that, as in many other words, the Scots have kept more cloſely to the orthography and pronunciation

CHRIST's KIRK ON THE GREEN. 149

The reird raife rudely with the rapps,
Quhen rungs war laid on riggs;
The wyfis came forth wi' crys and clapps;
Lo! quhair my lyking liggs!
Quoth thay, that day.

XV.

nunciation of the mother language, than moſt of the other northern dialects.

VER. 5. *Reird*] Or *Rerde*, for thus it ſhould be wrote; not as in Gibſon's edition *reir*. *Reirde* is properly clamour, noiſe, and ſhouting. Douglas, p. 300. 30.

"Bot the Trojanis raſit ane ſkry in the are,
"With *rerde* and clamour."——

And p. 37. 12.

"Syne the *reird* followed of the zounkeris of Troy."

Ruddiman derives it from Sax. *reod*, lingua, ſermo, as the primary idea ſeems to have been that of *ſhouting*. Hence, too, *rede*, council, advice. Teut. *raad*, concilium; *raden ſuadere*; Angl. *aread*, to pronounce.

Rapps] Stroak; alſo the ſound made by a ſtroak. Dougl. 301. 50.

"On bois helmes and ſcheildis the werely ſchot,
"Maid *rap* for *ràp*."——

And 143. 12.

"Als faſt as rane ſchoure *rappis* on the thak."

Alludit 'ραπιζω, percutio, ſays Rudd. who derives this from
hreppan,

hreppan, tangere. But, the truer etymon seems to be from Goth. *hropjan* clamare, from the *found* made by the *stroke*. In Suio. Goth. *rapp,* ictus; *gifwa en ett rapp,* to give one a blow; *rappa,* the verb, to draw or pull violenty. Ulphila, Mark ii. 23. *Raupjan abfa,* spicas vellere.

VER. 6. *Rung*] A rough pole.; Island. *runne,* saltus sylvæ.

Rigg] And *riggin,* the back bone. Goth. *rygg;* Ant. *rigg,* dorsum; Island. *hriggur;* Goth. *rigben,* spina dorsi. Notat etiam *dorsum* vel jugum montis; Gr. ῥάχις ὄρεος, the ridge of a hill. In Scot. the *riggin* of a house; Goth. *ryggknota,* spondilus, vertebræ; literally the *knots* of the back bone. Vide Ihre, Lex. in *rygg.*

VER. 8. *Likyng*] My beloved. Theotif. *likon,* placere; Sax. *lican, licigian, geleçan,* from Theot. *guodlichan, lik,* properly *corpus animatum.* Ulphila, Mark x. ver. 8. *Thanaseiths ni vind tua, ak* leik ain, They are no longer two, but one flesh, or one *body.* Hence *metaph,* for a lovely girl, Hawamaal Stroph. 84.

" Annad thotte mier ecke værna
" Enn vid thad *lik* liffa."
" Nil ego pulchrius cogitare potui,
" Quam illo corpore (puella) potiri."

Hence Douglas uses *likandlie,* for pleasantly, contentedly, p. 253. 14.

" Sae *likandlie* in peace and libertie,
" At eis his commoun pepil governit he."

Liggis] Lies on the ground. Ulphila *ligan,* to lie. Luke ii. 16. *Bigetan thata barn* ligando *in uzetin,* They found the babe lying in a manger. Isl. *liggia;* Al. *ligen;* Bel. *liggen;*

Suio-

XV.

Thay girnit and lute gird wi' granes,
Ilk goffip oder grieved,
Sum ftrak wi' ftings, fum gaddert ftains,
Sum fled and ill mifchevet.

The

Suio-Goth. calls *immoveable goods*, as lands, houfes, &c. *ligfa*; and *moveable*, *gangande fa*. In Scot. the immoveable wood of a mill is called the *lying graith*, in oppofition to the *moving* part, which we call *ganging graith*. Douglas, p. 462. 16.

———" They laid this Pallas zing
" Ligging thereon."———

STANZA XV.

VER. 1. *Girned*] Dentibus frendebant ut folent homines dolore iraque perciti. A. S. *gnirne*, indignatio, mœftitia. Cædmon 52. 19. Mid *gnirne*, cum quærimonia, indignatur. It is written alfo *gnorne*, mœftus, dejectus, qnærulus. Confer Lye, Gloff. Sax. in voce. The Saxon plainly flows from Goth. *knorra*, murmurare; Sax. *gnarren*, quod proprie (fays the elegant Ihre in Lex.) de canibus hirrientibus ufurpatur Ifl. *knurra*, to murmur. Olafs Sag. cap. 96. *Buender knurudu illa*; ruftici-murmurabant vehementer. *Knurla* and *kulla* denotes the murmur of the turtle dove. Vide Efdr. 38.

58. 14. Secundum hoc (says Ihre) *knorra* proprie erit, malis suis ingemiscere.

Gibson for *girned* reads *glowred*, which he rightly observes comes from Cimbr. *Att glora*, lippe prospectare; but we know not his authority here for this alteration. Adde Lye, in *Girnan*.

Lute gird] Gave hard strokes. Douglas uses *gird*, the verb, to signify *strike through*. *Throw gird*, did thrust through. Sax. *gird*, virga. Vid. Exod. iv. ver. 2. Matth. x. ver 10. Leg. Inæ. 67. Virgata terræ, *hoops* being made of rolls, before they were formed of iron. Hence Scots *gird*, fig. a hoop; and from it comes *girdle*. *Gird* to deceive or *beguile*, to go *about* one, *to take them in*. In this sense, Douglas, p. 219. 22.

" Was it not evin by ane *fenzet gird ;*"

i. e. false story, or trick. Alludit gyrus, gyrare, γυρος γυροω, says Ruddiman.

Granes] Groans. Douglas, *granyt*, groaned. The reader will observe in this verse the propensity of our old Scots poets to alliteration, a sort of ornament they seem fond of adopting as often as possible, and which was much in request with our Scandinavian ancestors, as we learn from Wormius de Litterat. Runica, and the poems of the ancient Skalds still remaining.

VER. 2. *Gossip*] Properly *godfather*, pater lustricus; Sax. *godsibbe*, cognatus ex parte dei. Vide Jun. in *Gossip*. " And " the child was called *Godbearn*," Godson. Chaucer, p. 209. 6. " And certes parentele is in two manners, either " ghostlie or fleshlie ; ghostly, as for to dele with his *godsib*." From the drinking on those occasions, the matres lustricæ, or godmothers, were called, in no very good acceptation,

Gossips ;

Goffips; and *to go a goffiping,* denoted a drinking match. And in this fenfe our poet here ufes it of thofe drunken clowns.

VER. 3. *Stings*] Poles, ftaves. Cimbr. *ftaung*; Plur. *fteingur,* hafta, contus, baculus. Angl. Bor. *Stangs.* Gib. Hence *nid ftang,* the fpear or pole of infamy, erected againft thofe who were called *nidingr, infamous.* In what this infamy confifted, (*nid,* fignifying *infamy* or *reproach*) fee in Ihre, Lex. voce *Niding*; and Jus Sueon. Vetuft. p. 346. which paffage Dr Robertfon has tranflated, Hiftory of Charles V. vol. I. chap. 5. p. 291. of the various ceremonies ufed in fetting up the fpear or *ftang* of infamy. Vide Bartolin. Ant. Dan. p. 97. feqq. Steph. in Sax. p. 116. Egill Skallagrim, the famous bard, deeming himfelf highly injured by King Eric Bloddox of Norway, who had profcribed him, refolved, before he left his dominions, to fet up the *nidftang,* or fpear of infamy, againft him. Having furprifed one of his villas by night, and killed one of Eric's fons, and feveral of his friends, with his own hand, juft before he fet fail for Iceland, " Confcenfa rupe quæ continentem fpectabat, " gerens haftile corylinum," (fays Torfæus, Hiftor. Nor. vol. II. p. 177.) " caput ei equinum affixit, formulam hu- " jufmodi præfatus; Hic ego haftam infamiæ (*nidftang*) ad- " verfus regem Eiricum et reginam Gunhildam ftatuo. Tunc " capite equino in continentem converfo, Converto, inquit, " has diras, in Genios qui hanc terram incolunt, ita ut omnes " incertis fedibus vagentur, nec quifquam eorum receptaculi " compos fiat, donec regem Eiricum et Gunhildam tota hac " terra ejecerint, et impreffa fiffuræ rupis hafta, litteris Runi- " cis hanc formulam incidit." The learned reader will at once fee the analogy of this ancient Scandinavian curfe, and that of the Romans, devoting others to the infernal gods.

U We

We have tranfcribed this curious paffage for two reafons. *Firſt,* It ferves to explain a term in one of our Englifh hiftorians, which our critics can make nothing of, though quite intelligible to thofe who know the meaning of the word *nidingr.* Matthew Paris, in his Hiftory of William Rufus, p. 12. 34. " Rex ira inflammatus, ftipendiarios milites fuos
" Anglos congregat, et abfq; mora, ut ad obfidionem veniant,
" jubet; nifi velint fub *nithing* nomine, quod latinè, *nequam*
" fonat, recenferi. Angli, qui nihil contumeliofius et vilius
" æftimant, quam hujufmodi ignominiofo vocabulo notari,"
&c. It is entertaining enough to fee Watts, the learned editor of this Monkifh Hiftory, gravely deducing this word from *nidth,* night. Nor has Spelman fucceeded better (Gloff. in *Niderling*) deriving it from *nid,* a neft, and *ling,* a chicken.
" Ac fi ignavi ifti homines (fays he) qui in exercitum pro-
" ficifci nolunt, pullorum inftar effent, qui de nido non aude-
" ant prodire." Would it not have been better for the learned Knight to own, that he did not underftand the phrafe? We hence, too, explain the phrafe *unnithing,* in the Annals of Waverly, anno 1088. " Rex Will. Junior mifit per to-
" tam Angliam, et mandavit ut qui cunq; foret *unnithing—*
" veniret ad eum." *Un,* privative, and *niding,* infamous; *i. e.* whoever was brave, and willing to fight.

The *fecond* motive for quoting particularly the paffage of Torfæus above, was to explain a cuftom ftill prevalent among the country people of Scotland, who oblige any man, who is fo unmanly as to beat his wife, to ride aftride on a long pole, borne by two men, through the village, as a mark of the higheft infamy. This they call *riding the ſtang;* and the perfon who has been thus treated feldom recovers his honour in the opinion of his neighbours. When they cannot lay hold of the culprit himfelf, they put fome young fellow on the

ſtang,

CHRIST's KIRK ON THE GREEN. 155

ſtang, or pole, who proclaims that it is not on his own account that he is thus treated, but on that of another perſon, whom he names.

We may obſerve here how common and familiar the Gothic was to the Engliſh, even in the eleventh century. Eric Bloddox being driven out of Norway, came with his Queen and Court to ſeek for protection from Athelſtan, who gave him Northumberland, anno 935. He lived much at York; and he and his people converſed familiarly with the Engliſh of that age, without needing an interpreter, as did his cotemporary Eigil Skallagrim, the bard, when in the ſervice of King Athelſtan. A century and an half before this period, we find the great Alfred entering familiarly into the Daniſh camp, and diverting them in the feigned character of a bard, without their ſuſpecting him to be a foreigner, which could not have happened, had his language differed from their own.

VER. 3. *Stanes*] Stones. Goth. *ſtains*; Sax. *ſtan*, lapis; Angl. Bor. *ſtean*, G.

The Iſlandic Spelling is *ſtain*. Thus, in all the Runic inſcriptions, *N. riſta ſtain*, N. erected this ſtone, *viz.* to the memory of ſome deceaſed perſon. Sometimes they write it *ſtein*. Worm. Monum. p. 245. Saſi ſati Runir *Stein*. Saſi Runicum lapidem poſuit.

VER. 4. *Miſchevet*] The verb from *miſchief*. The Gothic particle *miſs*, always implies defect, error, or ſomething bad; as miſtruſt, miſlead, miſcall, miſapply, &c. So the French *meſiant*, *mecontent*, *mecompter*, and the like. The Latins uſed *malè* in the ſame manner; *malèfidus*, *malèvalidus*, *effeminatus*. The Barb. Lat. Misfacere, malè agere, peccare. Confer Jun. in Gloſſ. Ulphil. p. 256. Iſl. *miſſater*, people who differ, among whom concord is wanting. *Misfoſſel*,

The menftral wan within twa wains,
That day fu' weil he prievit;
For he came hame wi' unbirs'd bains,
Quhair fechtars war mifchieved,
For evir that day.

XVI.

an abortion. Vide Ihre, Lex. in *Mifs. Mifftyrma*, malè et ignominiofè tractare. Bibl. Ifl. Judg. xix. ver. 26. *Og peir kiendu hennar, og miflyrmau henne alla pa nott.* They knew her, and abufed her all the night.

VER. 5. *Wan*] Got within, or betwixt two waggons. So Douglas ufes the phrafe, *Wan before*, He got before. Sax. *wendan*, to go; *wendan hidar ac thider*, to wander hither and thither. Vide Lye, in *Wendon*.

Wains] Contracted from *waggon*, as from the Sax. *wægen* is formed *wæn* and *weign*. Alam. *wagan*; Ifland. *vagn*; alludit ὀχειν, ὀχμα, vehiculum.

VER. 6. *Prievit*] Proved, found. Ifland. *profa*, to examine or try. Hence Sax. *profian*; id. *prof*, an experiment. Hence Germ. *prufen*; Fr. *preuve, eprouver*; Ang. *proof*. Kon. Styr. p. 14. *Prowa med fullom fkælom*, Prove by evident reafons. *Profshen*, a touchftone.

The pronunciation here belongs to the Scots; nor is it in ufe in any of the fifter dialects. Thus Douglas, Prol. to Book 10. p. 309.

" Thocht God be his awin creature to *prieve*."
To prieve fuch a difh, *i. e.* to tafte it.

VER.

XVI.

Heich Hutcheon wi' a hiffil ryfs,
To redd can throw them rummil;
He muddilt them down lyk ony myce,
He was nae baity bummyl.
                                    Thocht

VER. 7. *Unbirs'd*] Unbruifed bones. *Birr*, force, violence; alfo the noife an arrow makes in its flight. Douglas ufes thus the word *birrand*. Ifland. *bir*, ventus fecundus; *mier biriar*, oportet me. Hence Sax. *me byriad*, vel *gebyriad*; all which include the idea of force and ftrength: And this is furely a more natural etymology than that from *vir*, or *vires*, which the reader will find in Ruddiman's Gloffary. Confer Voff. Etymol. in *Brifa*. Cimbr. *brifim*, a bruife. Hefych. βριζει, πιεζει, ftringendo premit.

VER. 8. *Fechtars*] Here is another inftance of the old pronunciation retained by the Scots. Alam. *fehtan, vehtan*, to fight; and the Sax. *feohtan*.

STANZA XVI.

VER. 1. *Ryfs*] Bough, twig, or ftake. A. Cimbr. *Hriis*, quod virgam ramum, vel virgultum, fonat. *Vil eg tyfta hann med mannanna* hraife; Caftigabo eum cum virga virorum. Bibl. Ifl. 2 Sam. vii. 14. Hinc *hreifar* apud Ifland. loco virgultis obfita; et *breys*, virgultis confita domus, cafula. Danis
                                    quoq;

quoq; *Hriis foſtr*, eſt ſtrues e ramis arborum congeſta, et a *rice dyke*. Apud Anglos Sept. eſt ſepes ex cæſis ramis et virgis texta. Gib.
A. S. *hris*, vimen, frondes; Al. *ris*; Germ. *reis*; Hib. *ras*; Fen. *riſu*. Alludit ′pɪɟ vimen, ſays the learned Ihre, in *Ris*. Ulphila uſes *raus*, to ſignify a reed, which he and Wachter derive from *riſa*, ſurgere, in the ſame manner as the Latin *ſurculus*. Suio-Goth. *riſa*, virgis cædere; *riſ-bad*, verbera.

VER. 2. *Redd*] We cannot gueſs the Biſhop's meaning in his note on this word *red*; Sax. *to rath*, confeſtim, preſently. *To red*, in Scots, fig. to looſe, to unravel, or unfold. So Douglas, 127. 43.

" This being ſaid, commandis he every fere,
" Do *red* thair takillis, and ſtand hard by there gare."

Confer p. 339. 44. where *rede* fig. to make way. So we ſay, *To red the way*; to clear the way. To *rede* marches, ſettle boundaries betwixt contending parties; figuratively (as Rudd. obſerves) to make peace. To *redd* a fray; to inter-poſe betwixt two combatants; and often thoſe who do get *the redding ſtraik*, get a blow from one or other. Sax. *breddan*, liberare; *hriddan*, repellere. Hence Engl. To *rid* one's hand of a thing. *Riddance, raed*, expeditus; *reyden*, parare. Hence E. *ready*. Suio-Goth. *reda*, numerare, ſyno-nimous with *rækna*: Whence *reckon, reckoning*. Hence our *ready money*; and the Goth. *reda penningar*, id. But the Scots *redd*, as here uſed, comes immediately from *reda*, explicare, expedire, ordinare. *Reda ut ſit heir*, to comb out, or, as we ſay, to *redd* out the hair. Iſl. *greida*. Snor-ro, vol. I. p. 99. *Tha let Haraldur greida har ſit*; Tum Haraldus comam ſuam explicandum curavit; which, in conſequence of a vow, he had worn uncombed, till he ſhould become maſter of all Norway; Snorro, ubi ſup. Vide omnino Ihre

CHRIST's KIRK ON THE GREEN. 159

Ihre, in *Reda*. We fay alfo, to *rid* one out of the world, *i. e.* to kill him. So Knytling. Saga, p. 212. *Han red fwarba Plog*, He killed Plog the black. Snorro, voll. II. p. 245. *Ratha af lifi*, to red one out of life. And hence *rad*, flaughter.

VER. 2. *Rummyl*] Gibfon explains it of *thundering*; but this is a miftake, though he quotes that of Virgil, *Intonuere poli*, tranflated by Douglas:

" The firmament gan *rummyl*."

Properly it fig. to *rumble, grumble, roar,* or *bellow*. Douglas, p. 151. v. 7.

" Hillis and valis trimblit of thundir *rummyl*."

p. 200. v. 26.

" And landbirft *rumbland* rudely with fic bere,
" Sae loud nevir rummyft wyld lioun nor bere."

Suio-Goth. *ramla*, from the Ifland. *rymber*, murmur. *Rym*, verb, raucam voce edo.

VER. 3. *Muddilt*] Or *muddeled, i. e.* threw them down, fays Gibfon. Ifland. *mill*, in minutas particulas divido. Præterit. *mulde*, unde a *mill*, and to *mull*. Vide Hickes. Dictionar. Ifland. in *Mill*.

VER. 4. *Baity bummil*] Effeminate fellow. Gib.

It fhould be wrote *Batie*, that being a name our country people, in fome parts of Scotland, give to their dogs. The word *bummil* we remember not to have met with in any old writer. *Bulgia*, Goth. fig. intumefcere; *bula*, tumor; *bulna*, intumefcere. If thefe have any affinity with this word, the meaning may be, that he was no vain boafter—that he was not a *baty*, or dog, that would fnarl, but durft not bite.

VER.

Thocht he was wight, he was na' wyfs,
With fic jangleurs to jummil;
For frae his thoume they dang a fklyfs,
Quhyle he cried, Barlafummil!
I'm flain this day.

XVII.

VER. 5. *Wight*] We imagine the learned Bifhop has miftaken the fenfe of this word, explaining *weighty*, ftrong, ponderous, from Ifl. *wift*, libra, pondus. We rather deduce *wight* from Goth. *wig*, pugna, certamen. Unde Sax. *vig*, *vige*: hinc *vigian*, pugnare; *vigend*, bellator; Al. *wigand*, id. We find *vigan*, pugnare, employed by Ulphila, Luke iv. 31. Ifland. *wig*, pugna; Celt. *gwych*, vir ftrenuus, bellator. The elegant and accurate etymologift Ihre, juftly thinks he has here found the root of the old Latin *vicis*, as ufed for *pugna*; and that it was ufed in this fenfe, we have the teftimony of Servius, in his Notes to thefe words of Virgil, Æneid, 2. 433. Nec ullas vitaviffe *vices* Danaum. Hence, too, *pervicax*, quod *contentiofum* proprie notat. Ifidorus tells us, that the old Latins faid *vicam*, for victoriam. The Goddefs of Victory was called *Vica Pota*. Suio-Goth. *wega*, certare, cædere; *enwig*, certamen fingulare.

VER. 6. *Jangleurs*] Gibfon reads *jutors*, (we know not on what authority) which he explains from Cimbr. *Jodur*, Titan, gigas, Cyclops. To *jangle*, is to quarrel, gannire, blaterare, altercari, a Teut. *jancken*.

Jummil] Juftle. G.

Jummil] Collidere, infundere, in fe mutuo irruere; forte a *jump*, infilire, fays Skinner. Chaucer writes *jombre*; Germ. *jumpen*,

CHRIST's KIRK ON THE GREEN.

jumpen, micare, exilire. Sicambris, *gumpig*, lafcivus, fportful or playful.

Sklyce] Oftimes written *flyce*, from Ifland. *flita*, difrumpere, lacerare. Hence Sax. *flitan*, and Alaman. *flizzen*; idem. Otfrid, lib. 4. cap. 19. 29. of Caiaphas, *Sleizer fin ginnati*, He rent his clothes. Tatian, cap. 56. 7. *gifliz*, ruptura. Sax. *flyten* under, to flit and flice. Ulphila ufes *gafleithjan*, perdere, Mark viii. 36. Gafleitheith *fik faivalai feinai*, perdit animam fuam. Plura vide ap. illuftriff. Ihre in *Slita*. Ifland. *flyfs*, damnum, infortunium.

VER. 8. *Barlafummil*] Vox concertantium, nam in fingulari certamine apud Scotos, agonifta, ictu gravi læfus, portinus exclamat, *barlafummel*. Vox videtur deduci ex *bardla*, ictus, verber, et *fimbul*, grande, vehemens quid. G.

The original fignification of this word is to be found in the Suio-Goth. *famla*, which the learned Ihre interprets, Manibus ultro, citroq; pertentare, ut folent qui in tenebris obambulant. The Iflanders fay *falma*, which is certainly the original word, as Alaman. *folmo*, fig. the palm of the hand; and thus, in the paffage of Efaias (quoted by Ihre in *Famla*) Huner *wak himila finero folmo*, Quis ponderavit cœlos palmo fuo. Hence, too, the Lat. *palmus*; Ang. *palm* of the hand. Goth. *fumla*, manibus contrectare, attrectare; Fr. *patiner*, improbe contrectare; Belg. *fommelen*. To *fumble* (fays Jun. in Gloff. Angl.) proprie dicitur de iis, qui rem aliquam infcitè, infabrè tractant, quod Suecis eft *fumla*. Douglas feems to ufe *fumbler* to fignify a parafite, p. 482. 34.

" I am na caik *fumler*, full weil ye knaw."

Ruddiman here ingenioufly imagines *caik fumler* means a *cake-turner*, a fellow that will do any mean thing to get a bellyful; or an avaricious perfon, who *whumbles*, *i. e.* turns and hides his cake, left others fhould fhare with him. But

the

XVII.

Quhen that he faw his blude fae reid,
   To fle micht nae man let him;
He weind it had been for auld feid,
   He thocht ane cry'd, Haif at him.
                              He

the firft is certainly the beft interpretation. The other word *barla* is plainly derived from *parley*, a ftop or ceffation in order to fpeak. It was held ungenerous to refufe this of old, when demanded by one combatant of another. Hence we ufe the word *parley*, and to *beat a parley*, i. e. to make a fhort truce, in order to propofe terms of accommodation; and this phrafe is often ufed even by boys in their games. Or may we not fuppofe *barla* to be derived from, and a corruption of Suio-Goth. *barma*, mifereri? Chron. Ryth. p. 165.

    " Gud *barme* then omilde hempd
    " Deus mifereatur immitis vindictæ."

Ulphila has *armax*. Mark x. 48. *Armai mik*, Miferere mei. And this from *barm*, finus, ibid. Luke xvi. 22. quod quæ nobis indeliciis funt, in finu fæpe foveantur, fays the elegant Ihre (in *Barm*.) Hence Lat. *infinuare*, and our *infinuate*. Hence we may explain that unintelligible paffage in Auguftin, Epift. 178. Si licet, dicere non folum Barbaris lingua fua, fed etiam Romanis, *fi hora armen*, quod interpretatur, Domine miferere, &c. Lege, Si *Frauja* (or *Froja*) *armai*, Domine miferere; *Frauja* fignifying *Lord* in the Gothic. Vide Ulphila, Matth. xxvii. 63.

                                    STANZA

STANZA XVII.

VER. 2. *Let him*] Hinder or prevent. Sax. *lettan, gelettan;* orig. from Goth. *latjan,* tardare, morari. Hinc Ifland. *latur;* Al. *laz;* Dan. *lat;* and Angl. *late.* Alludit (fays Jun.) λnθομαι, Dor. λαθομαι, oblitus fum. This proves Junius's fondnefs for Greek derivations, where the originals are to be fought and found at home.

VER. 3. *Weind*] Thought or imagined. Gibfon here reads *trow'd,* which he rightly derives from the Sax. *truwian,* credere. *Ween* comes alfo from the fame fountain; *wenan,* exiftimare; Al. *wanen.* The root of all thefe is found in Ulphila's *wennyan,* or *wenjan,* or *gawenjan,* putare. Luke iii. 15. *Atwenjandein than alai managein,* exiftimante omni populo. Adde Luke vii. 43. Confer. Jun. in Gloff. Ulphil. *wenjan.* It is alfo ufed for *expectation,* becaufe this depends on *opinion; Thu is fa quimanda, thau antharanu wenjaima ?* Art thou he that fhould come, or look we for another? Luke vii. 19. Douglas, 222. 19.

" It ftands not fo as thou *wenys.*"

——*i. e.* thinkeft. He ufes *wenys* elfewhere for *tokens* and *figns,* as marks to point out the way, and determine our courfe. P. 100. 6.

" I knaw and felis the *wenys* and the way."

VER. 3. *Feid*] Enmity. Cimbr. *faide;* Sax. *fahth;* Lat. Barb. *faida, feida,* inimicitiæ; Angl. *fewd.* G.

Fec, Sax. inimicus; Ifland. *faad.* Hence *foe,* and *feud,* enmity. Leg. Athelftan, 20. *Sij he fa wid done Cyng,* Sit inimicus regis. In the Saxon laws, *fah* properly fignifies that capital enmity that fubfifted on account of murder com-

He gart his feit defend his heid,
  The far fairer it fet him;
Quhyle he was paſt out of all pleid,
  They ſould bene ſwift that gat him,
    Throw ſpeid that day.

XVIII.

mitted. Vide Jun. in Gloſſ, et Leg. Eccleſ. Canuti, 5, Spelman obſerves the ſame in voce *Faida*. This ſavage cuſtom of obliging the male relation to revenge the ſlaughter of his friend, is as ancient as any thing we know of the uſages of our Germanic anceſtors. "Suſcipere tam inimicitias (ſays "Tacit. de Mor. Germ.) ſeu patris, ſeu propinqui, quam ami-"citias, neceſſe eſt." Obſerve, it was not left to their choice, but under the moſt ſevere penalties they were *obliged*, to proſecute this vengeance, by every mean in their power. The exceſs of this barbarity at laſt brought on a cure, though the lapſe of many ages was neceſſary to ſoften the fierce manners of our anceſtors. We find many laws among the Salic, Langobard, and Francic ſtatutes, calculated to check this cuſtom; and King Edmund in England, about an. 944, complaining in one of his laws much of this evil, and ſuggeſting ſeveral remedies for it, and ordering compenſations to be made by the aggreſſor. However, we find it ſtill prevailing even in the Norman times; but how this inhumanity gradually loſt ground, and by degrees was annihilated, would lead us into a hiſtorical deduction, too extenſive for theſe notes, but we may perhaps give it in another work. Confer. Cange in *Faida*.

XVIII.

The town foutar in grief was bowdin,
  His wyfe hang at his waift;
His body was in blude a' browdin,
  He grain'd lyk ony ghaift.

Hir

Our poet here mentions *auld fied*; for thofe feuds of old ftanding, being fharpened by their progrefs from generation to generation, were, of all others, the moft deadly.

VER. 7. *Pleid*] Gibfon has totally miftaken the meaning of this word, explaining it by *reach*; getting beyond their reach. *Pleid* fignifies here the *quarrel, broil,* or *contention.* Thus Douglas, p. 111. v. 34.

—————" Bot gif the fatis but *pleid*,
" At my pleafure fuffered me life to leid."

Adde p. 454. 42. where it fignifies oppofition, controverfy. In Suio-Goth. *pleet*, ictus lævis; Sax. *plæt, handplætas,* ictus in vola. *Plætan,* ferire, unde Fr. *playe*; and the Bremen *pliete,* vulnus. Ifland. *plaaga,* cruciatus. Alludit πλητ]ω.

STANZA XVIII.

VER. 1. *Soutar*] Shoemaker. G.
The word *fhoe,* now in ufe, is foftened from the ancient Gothic *fko,* which is properly *tegmen,* (fays the learned Ihre)

id

id quod rem quamlibet tuetur—speciatim usurpatur pro eo quod extremitates munit, et specialissimè de indumento pedum. Leg. Dal. p. 15. *Skærper sko à foti,* si calceus pedem urit, *i. e.* If the necessity be very pressing. Ulphil. *skote,* shoes; Mark i. 7. Sax. *sco, schoh;* Island. *sko;* Aleman. *scù.* May it not come come from *skya,* tegere? unde *sky.*

————" quod *tegit* omnia, cælum."

As the Latin *nubes,* a *nubendo,* i. e. *tegendo.* Isl. *skyla,* to cover; *skysve,* tegmen. Whence the Scots *scoug,* a shade or cover; *under the scough of a tree.* Be this as it may, we find the Gothic *skaud,* a shoe, and *skauda raip,* shoes ropes; or, as we better pronounce, *raips,* i. e. shoe latchet. *Skohe is skaudaraip and bindan,* calceamentorum ejus corrigia solvere, Mark i. ver. 7. Alludit σκυ]ος, *corium,* says Junius; as if our Scythian ancestors had no name for a thong of leather, till they got it from Greece. If there is really any connection, the latter certainly comes from the former. *Skotwange,* the thongs or *whangs* of the shoes. *Gloves* are called in German *handschuk;* and, in some parts of Denmark, *boots* are called *knæsko.* Ihre observes, that Harpocration has the word Σκυθικος, which he explains ειδος τι ὑποδημαλος, genus calceamenti.

We find here the origin of the title, *Skosven,* an officer in the courts of the ancient Scandinavian monarchs. He was a kind of Lord or Gentleman of the Bedchamber, whose duty it was to give the King his shoes; but being always near his person, he was generally a rich and powerful courtier.

Thus, in Trygw. Saga, p. 2. p. 316. the rich Kali is called *Skosvein Einars,* though he was a man of great power, and a near relation of Einars.

Bowdin] So we think it should be read, and not as Gibson has it, *bowen,* which he explains as if it had been *boun,*

CHRIST's KIRK ON THE GREEN. 167

or *bowu, prepared to go,* from the Iflandic *bwen,* contr. *bun,* paratus.

Bowdin fignifies *filled, fwelled,* from Goth. *bulgia,* intumefcere. Kon. Styr. p. 212. *Ta wardir han giarnt trutin ooh bulgin,* Tum fere inflatur et intumefcit. *Bulgot,* flaccidum. Alludit Gr. βολοι, which the Gloffographers explain by φυμα]α, tumores. *Bulna,* intumefcere; *bula,* a tumor or fwelling raifed by a ftroke. A number of words are hence derived, which include the idea of *fwelling*; as *bolde,* ulcus, our word *bolfter; bolja,* a wave. *Bulla,* a fort of round bread ufed in Sweden ; whence the French *boulanger,* and our *bowl, bullet.* The Latin *bulla,* hung about children's necks, is alfo from it. Vide Juvenal Sat. 5. 164. Goth. *bulle,* poculum, Hiftor. Alex. M. ap. Litteratiff. Ihre in *Bulle.*

" Nappa och fwa alla *bulla.*"
Cyathos et omnia pocula.

Bullra, tumultuari, ftrepitum edere. Hence, too, *bolt,* a nail or pin, with a *large round head.* Ihre informs us, that the large wooden or iron cylinder, or roller, ufed for breaking the clods, is, in many places of Sweden, called *bult.*

VER. 3. *Browdin*] Browden, fwelled, or embroidered. Gib.

We find *browdin* in Douglas, which Rudd. explains *forward, bent*; and alfo *brudy,* abounding with; from *brood,* broody. Perhaps it may come from the Scots *bruche,* fignifying a gold chain, or bracelet, as if his body, ftreaked with his own blood, had appeared as if adorned with gold chains. Douglas, 146. 2.

" The *bruche* of gold or chene loupit in ringis,
" About thare hals doun to the breift hingis."

Vide ibid. 215. 25. Chaucer writes it *broche* or *brooch*; or

perhaps

Hir glitterand hair, that was sae gowden,
Sae hard in lufe him laift,
That for her fake he was nae zowden,
Seven myle that he was chaift,
    And mair that day.
        XIX.

perhaps from Sax. *brædan*, affare, De quo Lye, in Lex. Saxon.

VER. 4. *Grain'd*] Groaned. Douglas writes it *granyt*; Sax. *granan*; Cimbr. *grwn*, gemitus columbarum; Hibern. *gearan*, gemitus, querela. Alludit (fays Jun.) γρωνυς, explained by Hefych. τυς ακυονίας, και τυς μη λαλυίας, audientes, fed non loquentes.

Ghaift] Sprite. Sax. *gaft*, fpirit. G. Douglas writes it *gaift*, *gaifts*, which is nearer the Saxon orthography. Alam. *geift*. Hence Engl. *gaftly*, αγασος, ειδος αγασον, ap. Homer, which Euftathius explains εκπληκίικον, fpecies terribilis. Hence probably Scots *goufty*, ufed by Douglas, wafte, defolate, and lonely places, becaufe *ghofts* were thought to haunt fuch. Armor. *goafta*, vaftare, *to wafte*. I find in Lye *gaftoine*, ager incultus. Lat. Barb. *gaftina*, de qua vid. Cange, Gloff.

VER. 5. *Gowden*] Liquefcente. *l* in *w*, ex *golden*. Hinc *rufum* Scoti vocant *gowdy* locks, fcil. pro more gentium feptent. apud quas rutili et flavi capilli in maximo pretio habebantur. Hinc Cædmon vocat Saram, *Bryd blonden feax*, ponfam flavi comam. Lothum etiam appellat, *Blonden feax*; et in Edda Snorronis legimus Saturnum in taurum rutilum fe convertiffe, vertiſſe, cujus pilus quilibet aureo nitebat colore, *Var fagur gulz litur a huortu har.* Memnon etiam omnes anteiſſe pulchritudine dicitur, utpote cujus cæfaries fupra aurum nitebat, *Har hans var ſegra en gull.* Et uxor ejus fatidica, omnium formofiſſima, dicitur habuiſſe capillos *auro* fimiles, *Hun var alſtra Kuenna fogurſt har hennar var ſem gull.* Cap. 3. Præfat. Eddæ. Neq; mirandum quod feptentr. fcriptores rutilum cæfariem tot elogiis celebrant, cum multiplicem Gothorum nationem, Vandalos, Wifigothos, Gepidas, ipfofq; Gothos proprie fic dictos comas rutilos eſſe fcribit Procop. Hift. Vandal. lib. 1. Gib.

All the northern nations were remarkable for blue eyes, and yellow or fair hair. Of the Germans, *Tacit. Mor.* c. 4. " Truces et cæruli oculei, rutilæ comæ." *Juven. Sat.* 13.

" Cærulea quis ſtupuit Germani lumina? flavam
" Cæfariem."

Confer Cluver. Ger. Ant. p. 118. Ariſtot. Problem. fect. 14. 8. Conringius de Hab. Corp. Germ. p. 11. 12. From this mark, Tacitus (Vita Agricolæ, cap. 2.) infers the German origin of the Caledonians; " Rutilas Caledoniam " habitantium comas, et magnus artus Germanicam originem adfervaſſe." Lucan, Pharfal. l. 10. fpeaking of Cleopatra's flaves:

" Pars tam flavas gerit altera crines,
" Ut nullus Cæfar Rheni fe dicat in arvis
" Tam rutilas vidiſſe comas."——

So fond were the Germans of this colour of hair, that they uſed different ointments, both to give and to preferve this ornament; as Plin. informs us, lib. 28. cap. 12.

VER. 7. *Zowden*] So it ſtands in Ramſay's edition, but whether according to the M.S. we cannot fay; nor is the meaning of this word very eafy to difcover. In the Gloſſary

XIX.

The millar was of manly mak,
    To meit him was nae mows;
There dūrſt not ten cum him to tak,
    Sae noytit he thair pows.

The

to Ramſay's edition, we find *zolden*, explained *holden*. In Douglas we have *zoldin*, which ſeems to come neareſt the ſenſe here, ſignifying *yeilding*, or *yeilded*. But we think it better to own our ignorance, than to fill the page with idle conjectures.

STANZA XIX.

VER. 2. *To meit him*, &c.] Gibſon reads this verſe,

" With him it was nae mows."

Mows] Mockery, or jeſt. Thus Lindſay of Pitſcottie, of Sinclair, when the Lords ſeized him, " Is it *mows*, or earneſt, my Lords?" Battle of Harlaw, ſtan. 19.

" Their was nae *mowis* there them amang,
" Naithing was hard bot heavy knocks."

The French ſay, *Faire la moue*, to laugh at one; and hence Chaucer, Tr. lib. 4. 1. of Lady Fortune;

" And whan a wight is from her whele ithrow,
" Than laugheth ſhe, and *maketh him the mowe*."

Hib. *magam* illudere, deſidere; *magadh* irriſio, deriſus.

Mow

Mow alfo fignifies properly the *mouth*. Gothmund. Thus *faire la mowe*, is to diftort the mouth, as is done in looking contemptuoufly at any perfon. In Sui-Goth. *mopa*, illudere, vexare, Chron. Rythm. (apud Ihre in *Mopa*.)

" Jak feer Erik will ofs *mopa*.
" Video Ericum nobis illudere velle."

Our elegant etymologift remarks the affinity betwixt this and the Englifh *mope*.

Among the Ætolians, *mova* fignified *cantilena*, a fong; and in Celtic, *moues* denotes the fame thing. Hence *Mofai*, the *Mufes*, who made and fung verfes. Vide Pezron, Antiq; p. ad voc. Μῦϲαι. Μωκος, a *derider*, comes from the Celtic *moch*, a fow, from the action of that animal in turning his fnout up into the air, and men doing fo, as a gefture of contempt; μωκια, fannia, derifio; and the Celts fay, *moccio*, for *deriding*. Hence the French *moquer*, and our *mock*. Again, the ancient Gauls faid *gore*, for a *fow*. Hence γοριαω, irrideo, fubfanno; and from the fame origin, Χοιρος, fus. The ancient Scholiafts truly remark, that this word was *feminine*, among the ancient Greeks ; but they did not know the reafon, which is, that *gore* in the Celtic properly denotes *fus fæmina*, a *fow*.

VER. 3. *There durft not ten*] Gibfon reads the verfe thus:

" There durft nae tenfome thair him tak."

VER. 4. *Noytit*] Gibfon reads *cowed*. Goth. *nod*. neceffitas. Inde *noda*, cogere; *nodde*, coegit. Vide Gen. 53. v. 11. Ulphila, *Nauthjan*, uibi vid. Jun. Douglas ufes *noy* for hurt, annoy, and *noyfum*, hurtful, noxious. Thus pag. 191, 11.

" Sa fer as that thir *noyfum* bodyis cauld."

The buſchment hale about him brak,
And bikkert him wi' bows,
Syne traytorly behint his back
They hew'd him on the hows
   Behind, that day.

XX.

Ray (Collect. of words) obſerves, that in Lancaſhire they ſay *note*, to puſh, ſtrike, or gore with the horn, as a bull or ram. This he derives from the Sax. *Hnitan*, to puſh or gore, Exod. xxi. 28. Gif oxa *hnite*. And this from the Iſland. *Hniota* ferire, which is the true origin of our *noyt*. Vide Hick. Diction. Iſland. in *Hnyt*.

Pows.] So the Scots pronounce *Poll*, cacumen, vertex capitis. Hence to *poll at election*, to have each head reckoned; *poll-money*, capitation tax; a *pole* of ling, caput aſelli piſcis ſaliti. Skin.

VER. 5. *Buſchment*] Contracté from Fr. *embuſchement*, ambuſcade. We find *buſchement* uſed by Douglas. *Ambuſh* may perhaps be derived from *buſh*; and in woody places *ambuſhes* were generally placed. And this, too, is the opinion of Jun. Gloſſ. in *Ambuſhes*. Hence the Italian *imboſcate*, and the Lat. term *ſubſeſſores*, vid. Serv. ad Æneid v. ver. 498.

VER. 6. *Bikkert*] Laid a load of *rattling* blows on him. It would ſeem, that in this ſenſe the word is uſed in the old poem of *Chevy Chace*. Reliq. of Ancient Poet. vol. 1. p. 5.

 " Bomen *bickart* uppone the bent
 " With ther brow'd arras cleare."

i. e. their

XX.

Twa that war herdmen of the herd,
On udder ran lyk rams,
Then followit feymen, richt unaffeird
Bet on with barrow trams;

But

i. e. their arrows *rattled* in the quiver as they moved. In an old tranflation of Ovid, quoted in the Gloffary on this poem, we find thefe verfes :

"And on that flee Ulyffes head
"Sad curfes down does *bicker*."

Hence it came to fignify *fighting* or *fkirmifhing*; and here, fay our boys to each other, *Let us bicker,* i. e. *fkirmifh*.

VER. 8. *Hows*] The hams. *How*, from Angl. Sax. *hog* and *hoh;* and from this laft the Scots fay ftill *hoch*, as in Douglafs. Belg. *Haeffen*, verb to *hoch*, to cut the back finews of the leg, *fuffragines fuccidere*. Hence Jun. derives the phrafe, *hoxing* of dogs, *genu fciffio canum*. Adde Spelm. in *expeditare* canem. Ifland. *huka* ; incurvare fe modo cacantis. Perhaps, too, the *huckle-bone* had its name from hence. Belg. *hucken*, defidere, in terram fe fubmittere. Vide, Lye Addit. to Jun. Gloff.

STANZA XX.

VER. 1. *Herdmen*] Headfmen, G.

VER. 3. *Feymen*] Lege *faemen*, i. e. *enemies*. Douglas fometimes writes it *fa*, which is nearer to the Saxon *fah*,

inimicus;

inimicus; as from *feond*, fiend. Leg. Athelſtani R. 20. "Sy he *fa* with done lyng; *Sit inimicus regis.*" Vide LL. Edmundi R. 1. et Jun. Gloſſ. in *Foe*. From *fab* comes *feebld*, feud betwixt two families on account of the ſlaughter of a kinſman; Angl. *feud*; Iſland. *fead*; Dan. *feyd*. The Latins of the middle ages formed hence their *faida*, de qua Spelman in Archæol. B. Rhenanùs Rev. Germ. l. 2. p. 95. " *Faidam* vocabant Franci ſimultatem apertam, qua unus ali-
" quis uni vel pluribus bellum denuntiat. Ab hac Gallicani
" ſcribæ *faidoſum* appellat, qui *faidam* exercet. Germanis
" notum nimis vocabulum eſt." Every difference, however, was not called *faida*, but only that capital hatred which could not be appeaſed, but by the blood of the malefactor. Hence Gloſſ. *faida*, vindicta mortis. *Faidam* portare alicui, to declare private war againſt any perſon. The dreadful conſequences of this right of private war, and the numerous ſtatutes againſt it, are to be found in all the writers of the middle ages. See many curious particulars concerning it, ap. du Cange in *Faida*. Hence the poor Albigenſes, while cruelly perſecuted and murdered by the Papiſts, were called *Faididi*, quod profugi et exulantes erant.

Unaffeired] Unaffrighted, without fear, or as we ſpell it, *ſeir*.

VER. 4. *Barrow*] From Sax. *berewe*, which comes from Goth. *bairan*; Sax. *bæran*, *beoran*. Hence *bier*, on which the dead are carried; and thoſe who carry them are called *bearers*, and the ſpokes on which the coffin reſts, *bear-trees*.

Trams] Tram, or trum, is Gothic, and thus explained by the elegant and learned Ihre: " Pars arboris longioris in
" plures partes diſſectæ, ut commodius plauſtro injici queat."
Germ. *trumm*, fragorem; Iſland, *trumba*. With the German lawyers, *tramrecht*, or *traumrecht*, denotes that right
which

which one neighbour has of letting the beams or joists of his house into the nearest wall. Bohem. *tram*, trabs. Stadenius (Explicat. Vocum Bibl. p. 663.) obferves, that the Germ. *thramen* fignifies *beams*, and the crofs joists on which wooden ftairs are fupported, which leads us to the *thramfleins* of Ulphila, Mark i. v. 6. by which he tranflates the ακριδες of the Greek, which our verfion renders *locufts*, the food of John Baptift in the defert. Many of the ancients, as well as the Gothic Bifhop, underftand this paffage of the facred writer, not of locufts, but the tender tops of fome fhrub, or fpecies of plant, unknown to us; as Bengelius obferves in his note on this verfe; and therefore he deduces the laft part of the word from *teins*, virga, ramus tenerior. Adde Wachter in *Tram*.

May we not attempt, from what is faid of this word *tram*, to explain the word *flraba*, ufed by Jornandes, when defcribing the funeral of Attila Getica, cap. 39. " Poftquam " talibus lamentis eft defletus, *flrabam* fuper tumulum ejus, " ingenti commeffatione celebrant." Wormius (Mon. Dan. p. 36.) quotes a paffage from Plac. Lactant. ad Stat. Theb. lib. 12. in the following words: " Exuviis hoftium extruebatur " regibus mortuis pyra, quem ritum fepulturæ hodie quoque " Barbari fervare dicuntur, quem *flrabas* dicunt lingua fua." Now we know that nothing is more common among all the people of Gothic origin, than to put *f.* before their words. The word *trafwe*, the learned Ihre fays, " ufurpatur de " rebus quibufvis exaggeratis, *wed trafwe*, eft ftrues ligno- " rum," a *heap*, fuch as the funeral pile. *Trafwe* alfo denotes a heap of corn cut down; and hence our *thrave*, confifting of twenty-four fheaves, as we fhall more fully explain in our Gloffary of the ancient Scottifh Dialect; vide Ray's Collect. of Words, p. 75. Of this the barbarous Latin has made *trava, trava bladi*, de quo Cange. The cuftom of the Goths

drinking

But quhair thair gobs thay were ungeir'd,
They gat upon the gams;
Quhyl bludy barkit was thair bairds,
As they had worriet lamms
   Maiſt-lyk that day.

XXI.

drinking largely at the funeral of their chiefs, is too well known to need enlarging on in this place.

VER. 5. *Gobs*] Roſtrum, beak, uſed of birds of prey. Celtic, *gob*, roſtrum. Hence our *gab*, uſed to ſig. the mouth; and *gobble*, to devour greedily. Fr. *gober*. Junius obſerves, that the Gr. Καβλεω has ſome affinity to our words; and is explained by Heſychius, Κα]απινει, devorat, obſorbet.

Ungeird] Unprepared. Sax. *'gearwian*, præparare; and this comes from the Iſlandic *giora*, parare, facere. *Eg ſkal giora*, or *eg mun giora*; faciam, vel facturus ſum. Hickes (in Dict. Iſl.) thinks, that hence is derived the Scots to *gar*, to *oblige*, or *force* one to do a thing. *Gear*, Scot. *furniture*, *apparatus*. Iſland. *gearo, gearwe*, paratus.

VER. 6. *Gams*] The *gumms*; Teut. *gaum, gum*, palatum; A. S. *goma*, gingiva. Douglas 345. 31.

" His gredy *gammes* bedyis with the rede blude!"

Iſland. *gomur*, palatum. Theſe ſtrokes they got on the mouth explains what the poet adds, that their beards were all beſmeared with blood.

VER. 7. *Bludy barkit*] Gibſon, on what authority we
             know

XXI.

The wyves keift up a hideous zell,
Quhan all thir zounkers zokkit;
Als ferfs as ony fire-flauchts fell,
Freiks to the fields they flokkit.

The

know not, reads *bludy-burn;* the meaning of which we are ignorant of.

Barkned] Covered with congealed blood, as hard, and in the fame manner, as the bark covers the tree. Skinner derives *bark* from Teuton. *bergen,* tegere.

VER. 8. *Worried*] Worry, vexare, dilacerare, vide Lye, Gloff. Sax. in *Worian.* We find the original meaning of this word in the following paffage of Alfred's Verfion of Bede's Hift. Ecclef. l. 4. c. b. " Seo hreownes thæs oft ewedenan " woles feor & wide eal wees *worigende* & fornimende; *Sæpe* " *tempeftas dictæ cladis latè cunita depopulabatur.*" Such was the general fignification in the mother tongue; but in Scotch it is always reftricted to tearing with the teeth, as a dog does. Ray informs us, it is ufed in the fame fenfe in the north of England.

STANZA XXI.

VER. 1. *Keift*] Caft. Gibfon reads *gave.*
Zell] A doleful cry, indicating deep diftrefs. Sax. *gealpan;* jactare, gloriari, exclamare. The root is the Ifland. *giell,* vociferor; *gall,* vociforatus fum. We find in the

fame

same language *yle,* ejulo ; *ylde,* ejulavi. From *gielle* the Danes say, *at gielle,* resonare. Junius, in his idle fondness for Greek derivations, would bring it from ηλεμος, or ιαλεμος, cantio funebris. In the old English we also find *yawl,* lugubriter vociferari ; Island. *Gala,* vociferari ; Armor. *jala,* lamentari. If we must have a Greek derivation, may we not suppose it to come from αλαχαζω ? but it is needless to go from home on this occasion.

VER. 2. *Zounkers*] Young men, a Cimbr. *junkiære* (says Gibson) vel *jonkiere,* generosus vir juvenis. Goth. *jugga ;* and Island. *ung.* Hence Sax. *giung, jung ;* Welsh, *jevange,* or *jesange* ; Angl. *young,* inde *younker.*

Zokkit] Joined together in combat, as when oxen are joined together by the yoke. *Yoke,* from Sax. *geoc. joc.* ; and this from Goth. *gajuk,* Alam. *joch.* We cannot guess what the learned Gibson was thinking of, while he explains *yokkit,* ready to vomit. *Yoake,* in the north of England, sig. *to vomit ;* the *yoakes,* the hiccup. But sure this cannot be understood in this passage, as the true meaning. *Yex,* Angl. sig. singultire ; *yexing,* convulsio ventriculi ; Belg. *huckup* ; Suio-Goth. *hicka.* Confer. Jun. Gloss. *Hick.*

VER. 3. *Fire-flauchts*] Fire flying. Angl. Bor. fulgura *fire-flaughts,* vocant, G. And so do the Scots. The origin is from the Goth. *fleckra* and *fleckta,* motitare, from the quick and versatile motion of the lightning. Tobit. cap. 11. ver. 9. *Ta lopp hunden framfor at, och* fleckrade *med sin rumpo* ; Then the dog went before them, wagging his tail, Ezekiel xi. 22. *Ta* flecktade *cherubim med sinom wingom ;* Tum cherubim alas suas motitabant. Hence the English *flicker, flickering,* de quo vid. Jun. etymol. From this action of a dog fawning on his master, we find *fleckra,* adulari. Kon. Styr. p. 57. *Han sum ar falskr ok flikrar* ; Qui sub dolus est,

et

CHRIST's KIRK ON THE GREEN. 179

et adulatur. *Flikert* adulatio, ibid. p. 53. Alaman. *flecken*, adulari; *flechara*, adulatores. Hence Scot. *fleech*, to flatter. Douglas has *fleichand*, flattering, which Ruddiman, for want of a better etymon, derives from Lat. *flectere*.

VER. 4. *Freiks*] Bold, petulent fellows, who love to quarrel; alfo *foolish* and *impertinent*. Thus Douglas, Prol. to Æneid 8. p. 239.

" Ha, wald thou fecht quod the *freik*."

Teuton. *frech*, protervus, infolens, procax. Hence our *freak*, *frakish*, capricious. Suio-Goth. *fræk*, tumidus, infolens. *En freek uppfyn*, Vultus infolentiam præ fe ferens. Ifland. *fræckr*, infolence. Hence in Scots *fractious*, troublefome, quarrelfome. Gud. Andreæ Lex. Ifland. They fay alfo, *frækur*, *fævus*. Herraud's Saga, cap. 1. *Frækur i heimtum*, fævus in exactionibus. Knitlyng. 5. p. 8. *Oc var that ed fræknafta*, Erant hi milites fortiffimi. The learned and ingenious Ihre derives the Latin *ferox*, from the Goth. *fræks* or *fracks*, with great probability, in Lex. tom. 1. p. 585. This elegant writer alfo afferts (in voce *Frankrike*) that the Franks were called in the ancient language *Frakr*, from their ferocity. All the German writers agree in this. Gothofred. Viterb. Chron. part 17. in Proem. talking of the origin of the empire of the Franks, " Germani adverfus Alanos movent exercitum, eos vincunt, et " omnio extinguunt—et propter eandem victoriam a Valenti- " niano Imp. *Franci*, id eft *feroces* funt perpetuo appellati." Id. Catalog. Reg. Franc. " Poft modum ab Imperatore Va- " lentiniano vocati funt Franci, *i. e.* Feroces." And Ricardus Epifcop. tit. de Leone 3tio Imp. " Sed quia tempore Valen- " tiniani Imp. ejus mandato vicerunt Alanos, vocavit eos Fran- " cos, id eft *Feroces*." Rigordus in geftis Philippi Augufti, p. 74. " Quos cum multis poftmodum idem Valentinianus " præliis attentaffet, nec vincere potuiffet, proprio eos nomine

Z 2 " *Francos*,

The carlis with clubs did uder quell,
Quhyl blude at breifts out bokkit;
Sae rudely rang the common bell,
That a' the fteipill rokkit
For reid that day.

XXII.

" *Francos*, quafi *Ferancos*, *i. e.* Feroces appellavit." The reader will find more to the fame purpofe in Cange, voce *Francus*. *Frekner*, Ifland. fignifies *alacer*, ftrenuous. Olafr. Tryg. S. p. 2. pag. 298. *Tho at badi væri fterker oc frekner*, Quamvis robufti fimul et ftrenui effent. *Freki*, ferocia. Confer Ihre Lex. vol. 1. p. 586.

VER. 5. *Carlis*] Clowns; Sax. *Eorl* and *Georl*, Gib. The true origin is found in the Iflandic, not in the Saxon; for *corl* properly denotes a nobleman, whence *Earl*; but in the mother dialect, the Iflan. *Karl*, fig. a ruftic, or man of mean condition, as here. So too Alaman. *karl*. Voffius in Etymol. voce *Androfuces*, brings another etymology, but not a probable one. The Germans fay, *Ein hapfer karl*, a ftrong man. Hence too our *churle*, de qua vid. Jun. in voce, who obferves, that in the Sax. *ceorelboren* and *thegeaborn* are oppofed to each other; the firft fignifying a *plebeian*, the fecond a *gentleman*. It is from this idea of ftrength that the Englifh fay a *karlecat*, *carlehemp*, &c. *Carlifh* is clownifh, ruftic. Thus in the ancient ballad, the Childe of Elle, Reliq. of Anc. Poet. p. 112. vol. 1.

" And foremoft came the *carlifh* knight,
" Sir John of the north countraye."

Quell

Quell] Alam. *quellen*, Belg. *quellen*, domare, subigere. Sax. *cwellan*. It is used also to signify *killing*. Thus Douglas, 153. 50.

" Thre vilis tho', as was the auld manere
" In wourschip of Erix he bad doun quel."

and p. 263. 1.

" —— with this famyn rycht hand quellit and slane."

Hence *kweller*, carnifex.

VER. 6. *Bokkit*] Burst forth. *Bock* properly to *vomit*, and so used by Douglas. " Vox agro Lincolniensi familiaris" (says Skinner) " alludit Hispan. *bossar*, vomere ;" melius a Belg. *booken*, *boken*, pulsare.

VER. 8. *Rokkit*] Shaked. Rock a *cradle*; agitare, motitare cunas. Douglas 157. 30.

" How that the schyp did rok and tailzeve."

He elsewhere uses *rokkand* for rolling or tossing. Junius brings it from the Tuton. *rucken*, trahere, loco movere. But the true origin is from the Islandic *krocka*, (as also Ruddiman has observed in Gloss. to Douglas) cum impetu quodam moveri. It is ridiculous enough to find Mer. Causaubon going to the Greek ορyαζειν ανορyα)ει·, where there is not the smallest affinity of sound. Vide Hick. Dick. Island. in *Hrok*.

VER. 9. *Reid*] I suspect it should be *reird* or *rerde*, noise or clamour. Douglas, p. 300. v. 30.

" With *rerde* and clamour of blythness."

and p. 37. 12.

" Syne the *reird* followit of the zounkeris of Troy."

Confer ibid. 324. 25. Ruddiman brings it, with probability
enough,

XXII.

Be this Tam Tailor was in's gear,
When he heard the common bell;
Said, he wald mak them all a' fteir,
When he cam there himfell:

He

enough, from Sax. *reord*, lingua, fermo, as originally it denoted the *clamour of tongues*.

STANZA XXII.

VER. 1. *Gear*] Bifhop Gibfon obferves, that *gfor*, in the Iflandic, fignifies to *prepare*. True; but that has nothing to do with the word here ufed. *Gear*, in our ancient language, denotes all kind of goods and poffeffions, among which arms were reckoned by our warlike anceftors the moft valuable. Primarily it denoted a fheep fkin in the Iflandic;. and as that was the ufual garment ufed by onr forefathers, it was afterwards ufed to fignify *cloathing* in general; and hence *armour*, as we ftill fay a coat of armour. Vide our remarks on this word, Preface, p. 13.

VER. 3. *Steir*] The Englifh *ftir*, from the A. S. *ftyran*, movere. It is ufed here for violent commotion, as by Douglas, p. 34. ver. 53.

" But ardentlie behaldis all on *ftere*."

Junius

He went to fecht with fik a fear,
While to the erd he fell;
A wife that hit him to the grund
Wi' a grit knocking-mell
Feld him that day.

XXIII.

Junius has obferved the affinity betwixt this and the ſſυραχι-
ζειν, of Hefychius, to ftimulate or prick forward. Ulphila
has a fimilar verb, (only compounded) Mark xiv. ver. 5.
And—ſtauridedun tho, they murmured againſt her; where
fee the Gloſſary of Juuius.

Ver. 8. *Knocking-mell*] *Mell,* from the primitive *mal,* denoting force, power; and hence metaphorically what occafions
ſuffering, or evil. This is the meaning it carries in the oriental
dialects. Thus the Perfian *mall,* denotes anxiety, fuffering;
moul, patience; *malul,* difquiet; Arab. *mell,* patience; Celtic
mall, bad, corrupted. But this is not the place for thefe in-
veftigations, which we referve for our Scoto-Gothic Gloſſary.
Of the fame family with our *mell,* is the Fr. *mail, maillet;*
whence the Englifh *mallet.* The Latin *malleus* comes from
the fame origin.

Our poet here alludes to the large wooden beetle, made
ufe of by our anceftors, to bruife and take the outer hufk from
the barley, to fit it for the pot, before barley mills were in-
vented. This cuftom of *beeteling* the barley, has not ceafed
yet in fome places of the Highlands; and many of the hollow
ftones, ufed as the mortar, are ftill to be feen about our farmers yards, though they are no longer applied by them to the
former purpofe.

Mellis

XXIII.

When they had beirt like baited bulls,
And branewod brynt in bales,
They war as meik as ony mulis
That mangit ar wi' mails,
For

Mellie is, by our poets, ufed for *combat*, fighting. Life of Robert Bruce, p. 121.

" That men may by this *mellie* fee."

Douglas has it frequently. Fr. *melée;* whence the L. B. *melleia,* and *melletum;* and, from the Fr. Chaude, *mellée,* the barbarous writers of the middle ages formed their monftrous *calida melleia,* as Ruddiman has obferved. Vide Cange in *Melleia.* We have, too, in our old law books, *chaudmella.* Skene de Verb. Sig. though he knew nothing of the origin of the word, has rightly explained *melletum,* by ftrife, debate; as we fay that ane has *melled* or *tulzied* with ane uther.

Mell is ftill ufed in the north for a *mallet* or *beetle,* as Ray informs us.

VER. 9. *Felld*] From the Ifl. *fella,* to beat down. So the Englifh now apply it to trees, *to fell timber.* Alam. Fellen *befillan.* Junius's derivation of this word from *velt,* a field, is almoft as ridiculous as that of Cafaubon, who brings it from βεβλημενος ; and yet thefe men were etymologifts.

STANZA XXIII.

VER. 1. *Beirt*] Roared and fought with noife, like to that of bulls when baited with dogs. Douglas ufes the word *bere*

for

CHRIST's KIRK ON THE GREEN. 185

for crying or roaring. *Bere* and *birr*, according to Ray, fig. *force* or *might*; and in Cheſhire they ſay, *with aw my beer*, with all my force. In Scotland too we uſe this word *birr*, for might or ſtrength. Hib. *Baireadh*, quod effertur *baireak*, denotat fremitum, et *bairīm*, fremere.

In the old Engliſh we find *beray*, berayed with blood or dirt, befouled. Teuton. *bern*, merda. vid. Jun.

Baited] This word is ſtill in uſe, though its origin is not ſo generally known. With Chaucer *baye* is the ſtake to which the bear or bull is tied, in order to be baited. Plowm. T. ver. 87.

" As boiſtous as is bere at baye."

They then pronounced *baight*, which is now corrupted into *bait*. Chaucer, ibid. v. 588.

" He ſhall be *baighted* as a bere."

The root is the Iſlandic *beita*, agitare, incitare. Suio-Goth. *bekeya*, irretire, impedire. " Proprie dicitur" (ſays Ihre) " de " illis, quæ cancellis aut caveis incluſa ſunt."

VER. 2. *Branewod*] Roaring like madmen. *Braie*, fremere, vociferari, barrire, rudere. Hence Fr. *braire*. βραυωϛα Heſych. exponit κεκραγυια, vociferans. Lye deduces it from Cambr. *brevy*, to cry out. Douglas uſed *braithlie* for noiſy, ſounding.

Perhaps it ſhould be wrote *braynewode*, and then it will ſignify *mad*. Douglas uſes *brayne* by itſelf in this ſenſe, p. 438. ult.

" Quharfore this Turnus half, myndleſs and *brayne*, " Socht divers wentis to flie out throw the plane."

Brynt] From *bræn*, ardere; Goth. *brinnan*; Iſl. *ad brenna*; Aleman. *brennan*; Sax. *byrnan*. Hence amber is by the Dutch called *bernſteen*. Douglas uſes *brent* for *burned*.

A a *Bales*]

Bales] *Bale*, sorrow. Isl. *bal, bol,* malum; *bolua,* maledicere; *boluan,* maledictions. Douglas, 408. 2.

" Have reuthe and pitie of my wofull bale."
Chaucer, P. T. v. 68.

" Thou shalt be brent in *baleful* fire."
Gothic *baldwyan* torquere, Mark v. 7. *Ni balweys mis.* Do not torment us. Matth. viii. 29. *Quhampt hek faur mel* balwyan *unsis?* Art thou come to torment us before the time? Now Junius (ad voc.) properly observes, that the torment spoken of in the New Testament is always represented as by fire; hence the origin of the As. *beel,* rogus; Island. *baal,* incendium. Had we room here, we could prove hence the origin of *Beltyne,* the solemn fire kindled by our ancestors in May, at which time the Celts began their year. Vide Macpherson, Ant. p. 164. Smith Gaelic Ant. p. 31. Pennant's Tour, p. 94. From *tine* comes *tinder,* fomes; Alaman. *zundere,* item *tundre.*

VER. 4. *Mangit*] Ramsay interprets it *maimed* with carrying; Gibson reads *wearied* for *mangit*; Douglas sometimes writes it *menzeit,* confounded, marred, maimed. Thus of Andromache fainting, p. 78. 15.

" ―― to the ground all *mangit* fell echo doun."
and 440. 27.

" Bot then Turnus half *mangit* in affray."
Ruddiman brings it from S. *mangzie,* or *manzie*; Fr. *mehoign.* Hence, too, our *maim,* per contract. In our old lawbooks it is written *mainzie.* Reg. Majest. l. 4. c. 3. " He " quha is accusit in sic pleyes, may declyne battle, be reason of " an *manzie,* or of his age." From *mainzie,* the writers of the middle ages formed the barbarous Latin term *mahamium*;

though

For faintnefs thae forfochtin fulis
Fell down lyk flauchtir fails;
Frefh men cam in and hail'd the dulis,
And dang them down in dails
Bedeen that day.

XXIV.

though Ruddiman erroneoufly derives our word from it. Charta Henrici 2do. " Hæc omnia conceffi cum murdro, et morte " hominis, et plaga, et *mahalm*, et fanguine." Charta Philip 3. Req. Fr. ann. 1273. " Quòd percuffus membrum amitteret " feu vitam, vel etiam *mahainium* incurreret." Plura vide ap. Cange, in *Mahamium*.

Mails] Burdens.

VER. 5. *Forfochtin*] Wearied with fighting. G.. We obferve here, that in the Gothic dialects, and all its daughters, the particle *fore*, or *for*, increafes the fignification. Thus *hindre, forhindra,* impedire; *minfka, forminfka,* minuere; and often imports a worfe meaning than the original word. Thus *rakna* numerare; *forakna,* fig. to err in the fum. *Gora,* facere; *forgora* perimere. *Arbeta,* laborare; *for arbeta* fig. to overlabour one's felf. Hence too Engl. done, *foredone*; fworn, forfworn. In the Latin, *per* and *præ* have a fimilar meaning. So *oro, perero; facio, perficio; potens, præpotens,* &c.

VER. 6. *Flaughtir fails*] Thefe are the thin fod pared off the green furface of a field, with the inftrument now called a *breaft plough,* but anciently a *flaughter fpade,* which, as it were, *flays* the foil; from the Ifland. *ad flàa,* excoriare, cutem detrahere; Dan. *flae*; A. S. *beflæ,* excoriatus. Hence too *flakes of snow*, from their broad thin shape. Sax. *flacea*, floc- ci nivis. Alludit, Gr. φλοιος cortex, and φλοιοω, corticem aut pellem detraho; Sax. *flean*, to flea: Confer. Jun. Etymol. in *fell*. Ray says, that the surface of the earth, which they pare off to burn in Norfolk, is called *flags*. This sort of firing is still common in all the moorish countries of Scotland. The word *fale* or *feal*, turf, cespes, is found in Douglas's Virgil; and Ruddiman thinks that *feal* is only a contraction of *fewel*, as being a common kind of firing in Scotland.

VER. 7. *Hail'd*] To *hail*, Scot. is a phrase used at football, when the victors are said to *hail the ball*, i. e. to drive it beyond, or to the goal; and as they may thus be said to *cover* the goal, it may, perhaps, come from the Isl. *hill*, tego; *hulde*, texi; as this from the Gothic *huljan*, tegere, operiri. Matth. viii. 24. *Gahulith wairthan fram wegim*, Covered with the waves. Hence *hell* is called by Ulphila *halje*; as *theol*, hell, from *helen*, tegere, occultare. Thus *heal* in old English signifies *to conceal*, from Sax. *helan* celare. We call the husks of corn the *hull*, from the same origin. In Northumberland a *swine hull*, a sow house, or swine stye.

Duiles] The goal or boundary of the course. We imagine it comes from the Island. *duel*, moror, the stopping-place to which the ball was to be driven by the victorious party. *Dualde*, moratus sum; *duel*, mora. Hence *to dwell*, or make abode.

VER. 8. *Dang*] Perf. from *ding*, cedere, detrudere, to beat down, " Haud dubie," says Lye, " ab Hibern. *dingim*, " pellere, urgere." Douglas 229. 52.

" —— and with hir awin handis
" *Dang* up the zettis ——"

Teutoni *dringen*, from *ding*, *dint*, a stroak or blow; Sax. *dynt*, ictus. Infra St. seq.

" For

XXIV.

The bridegrom brought a pint of aile,
And bade the pyper drink it.
Drink it (quoth he), and it so staile;
A shrew me, if I think it.

The

" For he durst *ding* nane reddir."

Dails] In parties, eight or nine together; from Sax. *dæl*, a part or portion. Gib.

Vide Luke xv. 12. *Be dæle*, ex parte. Greg. Dialog. ex Vers. R. Alfredi, 2. 23. *Sume dæl*. partim. Thus too Chaucer uses it, Prol. to W. of B. Tale:

" But she was *some dele* deaf, and that was skaith."

Hence *dælan*, dividere, Luke xxii. 17. to give alms; *dæled*, divisus.

VER. 9. *Bedeen*] or *bedene*; for thus it is wrote by Douglas,

" Werpe all thir bodyis in the deep *bedene*." And
" How Æneas with the rout *bedene*."

This word is common also to the old English writers; Rudiman brings it from Germ. *bedienen*, præstare officium, *q. d.* assoon as desired.

STANZA XXIV.

VER. 4. *A shrew me*] So it stands in Gibson's edition. It should undoubtedly be read *beshrew me*, a very common

phrase

The bride her maidens stood near by,
   And said it was na blinked;
And Bartagasie, the bride sae gay,
   Upon him fast she winked,
            Full soon that day.

XXV.

When a' was dune, Dik with an aix
   Came furth to fell a fudder.
Quod he, quhair ar yon hangit smaiks,
   Richt now wald slain my brudder?
            His

phrase all over South and North Britain in the sixteenth century.

Though I have not Lord Hyndford's M. S. at hand, yet I do take this whole stanza to be an interpolation. It is not found in Ramsay's edition; and the language has something more modern in it than the rest of the poem. *Bartagasie*, a name (as far as I can learn) unknown in Scotland, strengthens the conjecture I have formed, that it is spurious. Whence the Bishop got it, I cannot say; but the whole of his orthography is so faulty and modern, that it appears he was but moderately acquainted with our Scottish idiom; and this has probably led him to think this stanza genuine, and to commit many errors in his notes on the poem itself.

STANZA XXV.

VER. 2. *Furth*] Gibson reads *out*; but we judge this the true reading, as it adds another letter to the alliteration of the
                                                            verse;

verse; an ornament, or rather jingle, our old poets were very fond of.

Fudder] A load, a great heap. Gibson writes it *fother*. Ray says it is commonly used speaking of lead, and expresses 8 pigs or 1600 weight. But *fudder* certainly means a cart load. Germ. *fuder*, et hoc fortè (says Skinner) a Teuton. *fuehren*, vehere, ducere. And this seems the true meaning of the word in this passage, though Ruddiman will have us to seek it in Hib. *fuidhre*, a servant or valet. We find *futhir* used by Douglas to signify a *trifle*, or thing of no value, p. 311. 29.

"I compt not of thir pagan goddis ane *futhir*."

But this has no connection with the other, nor are we to confound with it *foder*, signifying beasts meat, from *foda* nutrire; nor the Gothic *fodr*, signifying the sheath of a sword, used by Ulphila, John xviii. ver. 11. Hence A. S. *fodder*, *boge foddr*, a quiver, perhaps, because the first quivers and sheaths for swords were made of skins, as *foder* sig. vellus, pellis; Fr. *feutre*; Lat. barb. *fodrum*, de quo vid. Cange; Germ. *futher*; Angl. *fur*; confer. doctist. Ihre Lex. vol. 1, p. 511, 512.

VER. 3. *Smaiks*] *Smaik*, silly, pitiful fellow. Douglas, 239. 38.

"Quod I, *Smaik*, lat me slepe ——."

From Teuton. *schmach*, contumelia. Belg. *smade*. id Teut. *schmachlich*, contumeliosus. The root is the Isl. *smaa*, to contemn; *Eg smaae*, I despise; *smaa*, *smaar*, little, *small*, better pronounced, and nearer to the original, by the Scots *sma*; Goth. *smal*, gracilis, tenuis; *smalna*, gracilescere. Hence *smale* denotes the smaller cattle, as sheep and goats. Alam. call sheep, *smallfecho*. The ingenious etymologist Ihre

thinks

His wyfe bad him gae hame, Gib Glaiks,
 And fae did Meg his mudder;
He turn'd and gaif them baith their paiks,
 For he durſt ding nane udder,
   For feir that day.

thinks the Greek μηλα, *ſheep*, is nothing but the Gothic term wanting the *s*. *Smæda*, contumelia afficere; *ſmædeord*, convicia; Belg. *ſmaeden*, *ſmadden*, deturpare. And hence the words *ſmutſa*, *ſmeta*, *ſmitta*; unde Angl. *ſmitch*, and our *ſmit*, to infect or defile. In the parent dialect we find *ſmarede*, reculæ, minoris momenti res; *ſmaher*, vile, abject. Alfred. lib. 1. cap. 25. 10. *Smaher ſcale thin*, Vilis ſervus tuus. Iſl. *ſma hluter*, res viles; *ſmæcka*, minuere. Findur Norr. ap. Ihre, in voce. *Tok ſwa riki ad ſmæckaſt*, Incipiebant regna tum minui. Hence the true idea of the name given to Magnus, ſon of Eric king of Sweden, called in deriſion *Smæk*, not (as it is generally rendered) blanditiis delinitus, *flattered*; but denoting a weak, contemptible fellow, who allowed the whole province of Scania to be taken from him by the Danes, and thereby *ſmæckad*, diminiſhed his hereditary kingdom, contrary to the oath taken by the kings of Sweden when crowned. Vide Locceni, Hiſt. Suet. p. 106.

From this word *ſmæcka*, the barbarous Latin writers formed *ſmaccare*, to mutilate or maim, de qua vide Cange Gloſſ.

VER. 4. *Wald ſlain*] For would have ſlain. Gibſon reads, *that* hurt my brother.

VER. 5. *Glaicks*] An idle ſauntering prattler. *Glaffe*, or *glave*, is *ſmooth*, according to Ray. Hence *glavering* is uſed for *flattering*. In the Cheſhire dialect *glaver*, to flatter; A. S. *gliwer*, ſcurra, paraſitus; a *gliwan*, ſcurram agere, ſmooth.

Iſland,

CHRIST's KIRK ON THE GREEN. 179

Island. *glær* mare, from its clearness; and *gler*, vitrum Hence Fr. *glaire d' un œuf*, white of an egg; and Angl *giare*. Confer Jun. Etymol. in *glayre*.

VER. 7. *Paiks*] Blows, repeated strokes. Angl. *paice*, verbarare. I shall well *paie* him, I'll beat him. This is not to be confounded with *pay*, solvere debitum. Jun. derives *paie* from Greek παιειν, verberare ; but the true etymon. is from Cambr. *pwyo*, ferire, pulsare, percutere. In looking into the learned Ihre's Lex. we find *pak*, fustis ; and hence perhaps we have *paik*, to beat with a cudgel. Pezron Celt. Ant. takes notice of *bach* in the Celtic, sig. *fustis*. The Ang. Saxons, changing *c* into *t*, say *bat*. Fr. *baton*. Our most ingenious etymologist observes, that it is more than probable that the ancient Latins used *bacus* for a *stick* or *pole*, from the diminative *baculus*, still in common use.

We have thrown these notes hastily together, they being only meant, (as well as those on the Gaberlunzie-Man) as a kind of specimen to a Glossary of the ancient Scotish language we intend, at some future period, to publish, provided those who are the proper judges of such an undertaking, shall deem such a work useful for promoting the knowledge of the antiquities and language of our country.

F I N I S.

www.ingramcontent.com/pod-product-compliance
Lightning Source LLC
Chambersburg PA
CBHW032135160426
43197CB00008B/648